CURLY

CURLY

An Illustrated Biography of the
SUPERSTOOGE

JOAN HOWARD MAURER

CHICAGO
REVIEW
PRESS

An A Cappella Book

Originally published by Citadel Press
New edition published 2013 by Chicago Review Press Incorporated
814 North Franklin Street
Chicago, Illinois 60610

ISBN 978-1-61374-746-9

Library of Congress Cataloging-in-Publication Data
Maurer, Joan Howard.
    Curly : an illustrated biography of the superstooge / Joan Howard
Maurer ; [foreword by] Michael Jackson.
        pages cm
    Originally published: Secaucus, N.J. : Citadel Press, 1985.
    Summary: "While the Three Stooges were the longest active and most
productive comedy team in Hollywood, their artistic height coincided
with the years Curly was with them, and this is his definitive biography.
From 1932 to 1946 Curly was the zaniest of the Stooges, becoming
famous for his high-pitched voice, his "nyuk-nyuk-nyuk" and "why,
soitenly," and his astonishing athleticism. He was a true natural, an
untrained actor with a knack for improvisation, yet for decades, little
information about him was available. Curly's niece Joan Howard Maurer
amassed a wealth of Curly memorabilia—a mixture of written material
and rare photographs of Curly's family, films, and personal life—and
her exhaustive research and exclusive interviews resulted in this first
and only in-depth look at a crazy comedic genius. Plenty of intimate
details are included about his astonishing relationship with his mother,
his three marriages, and his interactions with his daughters and friends.
The book was so beloved among Three Stooges fans that it even garnered
a foreword from Michael Jackson, the King of Pop himself. This new,
redesigned edition of a timeless classic is sure to be appreciated by Three
Stooges fans new and old"— Provided by publisher.
    Includes filmography.
    ISBN 978-1-61374-746-9 (pbk.)
    1. Howard, Jerome Lester, 1903–1952.   2. Three Stooges (Comedy
team)   3. Comedians—United States—Biography.   I. Title.

PN2287.H725M38 2013
792.702'80922—dc23
[B]
                                                                        2013022098

Unless otherwise indicated, all images courtesy of the Moe Howard Collection
Cover design: Andrew Brozyna, AJB Design Inc.
Interior design: Scott Rattray

Printed in the United States of America
5 4 3 2 1

To my husband, Norman,
who convinced me I could do
the impossible
and then went about
helping me do it

CONTENTS

ACKNOWLEDGMENTS

I would like to express my deepest appreciation to the following people and institutions who helped me in illuminating my rather obscure picture of Curly's life:

Lester Borden, Columbia Pictures
Donovan Brandt
Eddie Brandt's Saturday Matinee
Candy Cole
Steve Cox
Elaine Diamond
Marilyn Ellman
Natalie and Tom Emery
Theodore Gell
Margie Golden
Ernestine Goldman
Dr. John Grenner
Jane, Frank, and Kelly Hanky
Dr. Bernice Herzog
Dr. Norman Howard
Paul Howard
Michael Jackson
Ruth Kramer
Jeff and Greg Lenburg
Irma Leveton
Brooklyn Historical Society
Stanley Marx
Rhonna Resnick
Dolly Sallin
Art Seid
Naomi Tepfer
Mrs. Milton Trager and the Trager Institute
Marc Wanamaker and the Bison Archives
Allan Wilson, my editor
Lyle and Carole Stuart

A special thank-you to all those fans who added their words of love for Curly:

Randall Beach
Joe Caruso
Gary Deeb
Margaret Engel, staff writer, *Washington Post*
Bill Gagan
Wayne Hawk
Linda Jett
Phil Kaplansky
Jack Kerouac
Steven Meltzer
Mark Pawlick
Barry Pearl
Peter Quinn
Scott Spiegel
Anson Williams
Steve Williams
Steve Zodtner

And to those artists who illustrated their love for the Stooges and Curly:

Bob Borges
Martin Garrity
Al Jackson
Wayne Koch
Tony Pecollo
Ralph Reichhold

PREFACE

In 1977, after I finished editing the autobiography of my father, Moe Howard, a thought came to me that a book should be written about Curly. After all, Moe and Larry had their biographies—why not Curly? He was the favorite among Stooges fans and, in fact, my uncle Curly was my favorite Stooge.

After mulling over the idea, I immediately put it out of my mind. There just wasn't enough information about this mysterious, crazy comedic genius. Curly, so I thought at the time, was a loner, except for his close relationship with my father—and my father was no longer around to be interviewed.

Through the years, without giving it much thought, I found myself collecting bits and pieces about Curly and tucking them away. Eight years later, while going through my over-flowing files to make room for current projects, I rediscovered my mélange of Curly memora-bilia—bulging folders of fascinating written material and wonderful photographs. But I knew there was still not enough information to complete an in-depth book on this favorite Stooge. I then made my decision. If I was to write a book on my uncle, I would have to find more facts and photographs.

My first thought was to call my cousin Dr. Norman Howard, who I remembered had vis-ited Curly in California several times in the '40s and actually lived with him during his Colum-bia days when Curly was in his prime. I interviewed Norman for several days and uncovered an abundance of fascinating and humorous Curly data that I was previously unaware of.

My next contact was with Norman's sister, Dr. Bernice Herzog, a cousin whom I hadn't spoken to in years. I remembered that Curly, in the '20s, visited with her parents in Pittsburgh and lived in their home. I wrote Bernice and was both delighted and amazed at the letter I received, crammed with new information about Curly's youth before he became a film star.

Additional information about Curly came from Bernice's sister, my cousin Dolly Sallin, who lives here in Los Angeles. Encouraged, I jumped into my sleuthing full tilt and dropped a line to my second cousin Emily Trager, who had just moved from Hawaii to California. Emily called me, and we made plans to have lunch together in Palm Springs, where she was spending her vacation. The interview was fruitful, but the importance of our meeting was not revealed until just before I left, when she handed me an envelope filled with old family photographs. Among them was a fascinating picture of Curly in the '20s, returning from a trip to Paris, decked out in the latest in high fashion, sporting a waxed mustache and flanked by his mother and father—my grandparents.

As there were still many missing pieces to the puzzle of Curly's life during the '30s and '40s, I decided to get in touch with Elaine Diamond, Curly's second wife, and her daughter Marilyn. I had been estranged from most of the members of this side of my family due to Curly's divorces and my father's habit of drawing away from each of Curly's wives after Curly separated from them. However, I had intermittently kept in touch with my Aunt Elaine and my cousin Marilyn, Curly's first daughter. I called them both, and they were very excited over the idea of a book about Curly and agreed to help me. But I hesitated about calling Curly's other daughter, my cousin Janie, whom I last saw in 1948 when she was an infant. I wondered what she might think and feel after all these years with nary a word from her first cousin. But Janie's input was vital if the book was to be complete, and it was mandatory that I speak with her about her childhood spent with Curly. I gathered up the courage and called.

My telephoning Janie from out of the blue caught her completely off guard, but in spite of this and our decades of estrangement, she and her husband, Frank, were extremely warm and friendly, and after agreeing to help me with the book, Janie put me in touch with her mother's sister, Natalie Emery. Valerie, Janie's mother and Curly's fourth wife, had died almost twenty years prior. Janie was certain that Natalie could be very helpful to me and would fill in that period of Curly's life after his marriage to her mother. Natalie was wonderful, and even though it was a difficult part of her life to look back on, she never flinched as I asked her many trying and personal questions.

After several weeks, I had interviewed everyone I could think of who had even the minutest contact with Curly, and they had sent on their wonderful photographic collections. I finally put together my presentation for Citadel Press, selected a representative assortment of wonderful old photographs and illustrations, and sent it off.

Then I sat back, expecting what all authors always anticipate will occur after a submission—a lengthy wait for the publisher's approval or rejection. I was absolutely flabbergasted when, forty-eight hours later, my husband came into the yard, where I was gardening, and asked me, "What do you want first, the good news or the bad news?" I had no idea what he was talking about, but I bit and asked for the good news first. "The good news," Norman said, "is that Citadel wants to publish the Curly book; the bad news is it has to be finished in ninety days in order to make their fall schedule." Norman paused and added, "Don't worry—I'll help you."

"Don't worry" had been Norman's cry for more than a quarter century. Norman was a "leave it to the last minute" guy, while I'm a "get it done yesterday" girl. Between Norman's constant procrastination during the writing of this book and the constant banging, sawing, and hammering of the major remodeling under way in our house, I was certain that meeting the book's tight deadline would be a total impossibility.

Despite the horrific working conditions, we both shut our eyes and plunged ahead and somehow managed to meet the deadline.

When it came time to decide on a choice for someone to write the book's foreword, I recalled that I had recently seen an article in *People* magazine on the rock star Michael Jackson. In the article there was a double-page spread with a photograph of his dressing table, captioned "Some of Michael's favorite things." Prominent on the table was a picture of the Three Stooges, and I instantly realized that *the* Michael Jackson was a Three Stooges fan. I wrote him and asked if he would write the foreword for the book and was truly surprised when, without hesitation, he took time from his busy schedule to get word to me that he would consider it an honor.

To track down the information for the first chapter, "Curly's Roots," I dug deeply into my voluminous Three Stooges files and located over one hundred typed pages that were deleted from my father's autobiography. These pages consisted of the actual bedtime stories told to Moe by his father, which set forth every detail of my grandfather's arduous trip from Russia to America with his new wife, Jennie. My files also contained an assortment of old family letters from Moe to Curly with facts about the early history of the Stooges' vaudeville act as well as details of Moe's many experiences with his brothers Shemp and Curly when they were children in Brooklyn and growing up together. My attic, a virtual catch-all with cartons of Stooges memorabilia, gave up more of its secrets, including hundreds of personal letters from fans that my father had saved throughout the years, many old photographs, and hundreds of faded newspaper clippings. In searching through dozens of file drawers and cardboard cartons, I also rediscovered my mother's family album, which she started back in the early '20s and which was crammed with personal notations that documented the careers of all the Stooges for several decades.

The interlocking of the puzzle pieces of Curly's life was accelerated when, in mid-1984, I received what I thought was just another fan letter but was surprised to find this one starting "Dear Cousin" and ending with "Sincerely, Stanley Marx." Stanley was, indeed, a long-lost cousin from Brooklyn, and his help in uncovering new Curly facts and photos was invaluable. Stanley supplied vintage family photographs, took time off from his real estate business to research fresh, new anecdotes about Curly's parents, Jennie and Solomon, and conducted a search through the New York City Department of Records for Curly's marriage licenses as well as his birth certificate. He also found several wonderful old photographs of the Bensonhurst area in the archives of the Long Island Historical Society (now the Brooklyn Historical Society), which helped to set the scene for the chapter on Curly's childhood. When I asked him for his thoughts about Curly, he sent on a wonderful letter, and much of it was used in the chapter titled "Aftermath." For all his help, I owe Stanley much more than mere thanks.

And then there were the many non-kindred fans whom I wrote to requesting their thoughts about Curly. They all came through, sending on words about their favorite Stooge that were both warm and wonderful.

From the very beginning of my commitment to writing a comprehensive book on my uncle Curly, I had my heart set on finding someone to do a psychological profile on this special

Stooge. My longtime friend Dr. John Grenner agreed to help me, and it was John's suggestion that we do our profile in question-and-answer form. This unusual look into Curly's psyche became a separate chapter in the book, titled "What Made Curly Tick?"

Writing *Curly* has been the most exciting experience of my career and has given me the welcome chance to get back together with much of my family.

For more than half a century, the on-screen Curly has been in the public eye and has been loved by millions. It is my sincerest hope that the readers of this book will find the offscreen Curly equally engaging, that they will understand the many problems faced by this complex human being, and that one and all will have as much enjoyment in reading about him as I have had in writing about him.

CURLY'S FAMILY TREE

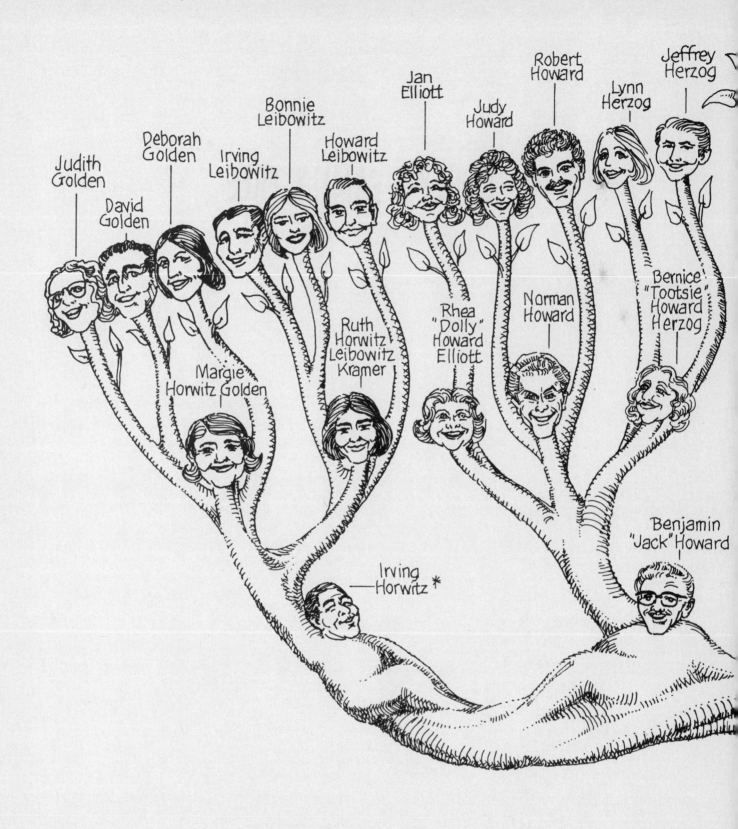

Judith Golden

David Golden

Deborah Golden

Irving Leibowitz

Bonnie Leibowitz

Howard Leibowitz

Jan Elliott

Judy Howard

Robert Howard

Lynn Herzog

Jeffrey Herzog

Margie Horwitz Golden

Ruth Horwitz Leibowitz Kramer

Rhea "Dolly" Howard Elliott

Norman Howard

Bernice "Tootsie" Howard Herzog

Irving Horwitz *

Benjamin "Jack" Howard

* Irving Horwitz was the only brother who did not change his name to Howard.

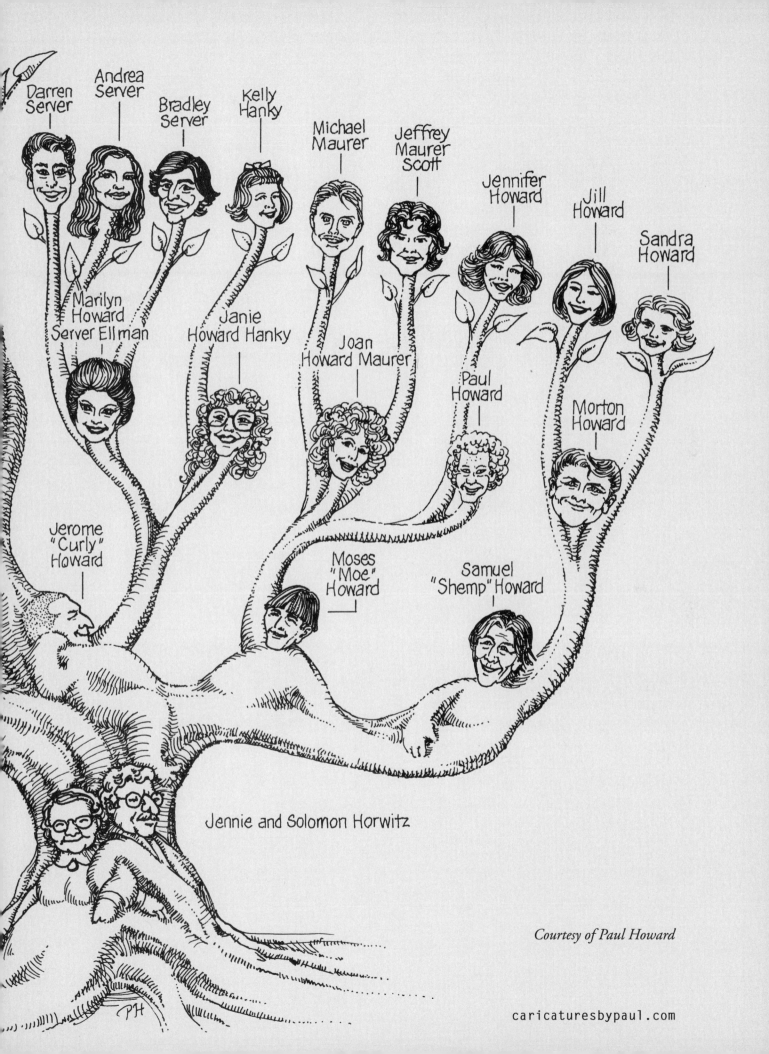

Courtesy of Paul Howard

caricaturesbypaul.com

1

CURLY'S ROOTS (1886–1903)

Curly's Parents Start the Stooge Dynasty • Life with Father, Mother, Moe, and Shemp

Shortly after the turn of the century, my father, Moe Howard, who was a very young child at the time, listened with fascination to his father, Solomon, as he told him bedtime stories about his youth in Russia and his emigration to America.

Decades later, in the late '60s and early '70s, Moe, whose retentive memory was spectacular, decided to write his autobiography and jotted down, in the minutest detail, his memories

Kovno (Kaunas), Lithuania, where Curly's father, Sol Horwitz, was born.

World Book Encyclopedia

of those ancient bedtime stories. In the first segment of his original manuscript, there were hundreds of pages covering just my grandfather meeting my grandmother and hundreds more detailing their arduous journey from Russia to America.

After my father died, the task of editing those voluminous notes down to size and completing his autobiography fell on my shoulders, and hundreds of pages of the Horwitz family's ancestry were deleted.

Ten years later, while researching the mystery of Curly and his roots, I came across this mass of discarded material tucked away in a carton in my attic. Knowing that no book on my uncle Curly, the superstooge, would be complete without more details about his family, I found myself rereading page after page.

This is no ordinary story but a yarn that has the makings of a "Jewish *Roots*" and that describes where all the Stooges' insanity originated.

Curly's father, Solomon Gorovitz, was born in the city of Kovno (Kaunas), Lithuania, on November 4, 1872. At age fifteen, as was the tradition for orthodox Jewish youths, Solomon, shy and inexperienced, was sent to a rabbinical seminary over one hundred miles away in Vilna (Vilnius), where he would live at his cousin's house during the two years of his biblical studies.

Taking along a few simple belongings, young Solomon made the difficult journey by foot, wagon, and train. To this wide-eyed, naive Lithuanian teenager, the trip and the radical changes in his life loomed as a frightening event.

Upon his arrival, Solomon breathed an exhausted sigh of relief when he was greeted by his cousin Nathan and then taken by horse and buggy to the Gorovitz home. It was here he met his second cousin, Jennie. Born on April 4, 1869, Jennie Gorovitz was three years older than

Solomon. She was robust, with sparkling eyes and raven-black hair, a young girl who could be sweet as an angel one minute and a domineering martinet the next.

To Jennie, Solomon was far from being the boy every teenage girl dreams about. As the weeks passed, Solomon was bewildered by her scorn until another cousin, Victor, explained, "Don't you know that you hurt most the people you love."

Cousin Victor's words helped to soothe Solomon's wounded pride for the moment, but throughout his life my grandfather learned to totally ignore most of Jennie's barbs, except those times when they became too thorny. Then he'd put on his hat, show her his back, and stride silently out the door. In later years, Curly, Moe, and Shemp referred to this as "the hat trick."

Later, as Solomon's graduation from rabbinical school drew near, fate stepped in to change his life forever. My great-grandfather had gotten word that the czar's soldiers were roaming the country and conscripting all men of Solomon's age into the Russian army.

To a religious Jewish family, the thought was intolerable, since Jewish boys were conscripted for incredible lengths of service and sometimes subjected to forced conversions.

This was a time of urgency, and the Gorovitzes had to take immediate action. They decided to give Solomon the identification papers of a young Jewish man who had died after serving his stint in the army. Aware that this ruse was certain to be discovered eventually, the Gorovitzes made plans to get Solomon out of the country and ship him to America.

Eastern Europe in the nineteenth century. *Map by Norman Maurer*

This was easier said than done. The Gorovitzes realized that naive, unworldly Sol would never survive the difficult journey alone. On the other hand, Jennie was a strong, strapping young woman, and the two together would have more than a fighting chance to make it out of the country, but they had to patch up their differences, marry immediately, and leave for America together.

Opposites attract, and Mrs. Gorovitz, always the optimist, was certain Sol and Jennie would eventually learn to love each other.

But Jennie had a mind of her own, and it took some convincing to get her to agree to the marriage. The wedding was a hurried one, and immediately after the ceremony, my great-grandmother and -grandfather made preparations to send the newlyweds on their way.

Jennie's bag was packed, and the senior Gorovitzes supplied the young couple with enough kopecks and rubles to cover the costs of lodging as well as bribes for the border guards and payment for passage to America. Mr. Gorovitz, however, was adamant about securing Jennie's dowry, since the couple would need the money from it when they got to America. He placed one hundred rubles in a small sack and concealed it by sewing it inside the fly of Solomon's pants. Little did he or Solomon realize the embarrassment that would result from this simple security measure.

And so our young couple joined several other young couples for their difficult trek across Lithuania, Poland, and Germany, finally arriving at their destination, the North Sea port of Hamburg.

They were packed like sardines in the ship's steerage, and the voyage across the Atlantic lasted fourteen days. The seas were rough and, as was always the case in steerage, the trip was most unpleasant. This was especially so for Solomon, who constantly held his hands to his fly to protect his wife's dowry; he had to endure with embarrassment the curious stares of his fellow passengers.

During the voyage, Jennie made detailed plans of how she would find work in America. Even at this early point in their married life, Jennie demonstrated that she was destined to take over as the family breadwinner.

The trip across Europe under Jennie's guidance had taught Solomon respect for her capabilities and her honesty, qualities that he greatly admired. Neither a thinker nor a man of action, he surrendered his masculine authority then as he would continue to do throughout his life.

Upon the young Gorovitzes' arrival at Castle Garden, New York, in 1890, they went through the usual immigration red tape and the typical problems caused by the ever-present language barriers. When asked their names by the immigration officer, Jennie, with her thick Lithuanian accent, replied, "Gorovitz." To the officer it sounded like "Horwitz," and Horwitz it would remain for the rest of their lives. Not so with Moe, Shemp, Curly, and Jack, who, for the sake of euphony, would eventually change their name to Howard.

Jennie's oldest brother, Julius, who had previously emigrated to America, gave the newly-weds the first roof over their heads—a room in his furnished apartment at Twenty-Second Street and Third Avenue.

Curly's fraternal grandparents in Europe, circa 1880. Chaim Nocham (Charles Norman) was born and died in a shtetl near Vilna, killed while rescuing the Torah from the town synagogue in 1900. Wife Dora died of starvation in a post–World War I famine in Russia.

Courtesy of Stanley Marx

There they were, Jennie and Sol, two strangers in a strange land, unaware that they would one day change the course of comedic history.

Jennie and Solomon started their family in 1891 with the birth of a son, Irving, a sickly child but nevertheless a joy because of the added realization that, according to law, Irving was an instant American citizen. Jennie and Sol catered to their new son's every whim, since he was their firstborn and tradition gave him a special place in this blossoming Jewish family.

Irving, however, would one day be Jennie's first disappointment, for he would grow up to become an insurance salesman and not the professional that Jennie, the typical Jewish mother, had dreamed about.

In 1892 Sol found a job as a clothing cutter. He worked hard until the union struck for a shorter work week and he found himself unemployed. Desperate to prove that he could support his family, he decided to go into business for himself. He used every cent of his and Jennie's money to purchase a pack of notions, which consisted of handkerchiefs, socks, matches, and other sundries, and made the decision to become a peddler.

Jennie hated the idea of a husband who was a peddler, but she had little choice. Irving's delicate constitution forced her to stay home and care for him, but Jennie wasn't too concerned about her husband's new career, as she had the feeling that Sol's current vocation would be short-lived. She was right.

One morning, while hawking his wares on a Brooklyn street, Sol was accosted by a group of toughs who had decided to harass this "Jewish character" with the fiery red mustache and bulging backpack. They went after Sol, pulling his mustache, roughing him up, and finally shoving him hard against a nearby wall. The impact ignited one of the matchboxes in his backpack. Instead of ripping off the pack, Sol panicked and ran down the street, his back in flames. Fortunately, onlookers in the windows above heard his cries and doused him with whatever liquids they could find, including buckets of slop.

Poor Sol limped his way home, arriving flushed, beaten, and filthy. Sympathetic, Jennie took him in her arms, then helped him clean up. She realized that Sol would never change, that he would always be that young, inexperienced boy from Vilna who wanted to be a rabbi. She knew from that moment on that she would have to take charge in order to keep a roof over her family's heads and food on their table.

Through the years, Jennie accepted the job of provider with graciousness, skill, and enthusiasm. She thrived on accomplishment and constantly tried to make Sol feel that he had contributed to her success. Even when she became a wealthy real estate saleswoman, consummating million-dollar deals, she would always hand Sol the checks for deposit—made out in his name. In her own strange way, she had grown to love and honor this man she called her husband.

In 1893 Jennie gave birth to another son, Benjamin "Jack," a fat little blond-haired baby. Although Jack would be a good student and a fine athlete, he would not be the answer to Jennie's dream of having a professional in the family, for he would follow in his brother Irving's footsteps and become an insurance salesman.

While Jack was the picture of health and vitality, Irving, now two, was thin and short for his age. Although Jennie admired and doted on her new curly-haired, blue-eyed son, she drew ever closer to Irving, whom she felt needed her more.

It wasn't until 1895 that Jennie's first comedian son came along. On March 17 Samuel "Shemp" Horwitz was born. How his name evolved to Shemp is a family classic. Once again it was Jennie's European accent that caused the dilemma. When she would call "Sam," it sounded to others like "Sams" and sometimes like "Shemps," and among the Horwitz boys and their friends, that strange name stuck.

Shemp was a stubborn child. If he fell or hurt himself or did something wrong and was punished, he would never cry, just tighten his lips, clench his teeth, and rarely utter a sound. As he grew older, this would change, and during his school days Shemp would make up for his childhood silence by becoming the most mischievous and gregarious kid in the neighborhood.

Neither athletically inclined nor a good student, Shemp's favorite pastime throughout grammar school was making comical faces at his fellow students and his teachers and draw-

Curly's brothers, circa 1900: Moe in front row; second row, left
to right, Jack, Irving, and Shemp.

ing funny pictures. He was continually clowning and would do anything and everything for a laugh, which resulted in Jennie spending as much time in school as Shemp did.

On the day of Shemp's graduation from elementary school, Jennie and Sol watched proudly as their son stepped up on the platform. As the principal handed Shemp his diploma, he grinned and said, "Students, ladies and gentlemen, this young man did not graduate . . . his mother did."

In the year 1897 two momentous events occurred in the lives of the Horwitzes. First, thanks to Jennie's success in real estate, the family moved to Bath Beach, a lovely summer resort in the Bensonhurst area of Brooklyn. Their new house had a wonderful yard filled with large shade trees under which Sol relaxed and Irving, Jack, and Shemp romped about.

The neighborhood consisted mainly of Irish Catholics, and when the Horwitzes moved in, there were only seven Jewish families living in the area. This was no deterrent to Jennie and Sol. Jennie was excited about the neighborhood's real estate potential, and Sol was delighted that there was a synagogue nearby.

Bath Beach was to have a tremendous influence on the Horwitz boys. The area had a great many residents in the theatrical profession, and within a mile from Sol and Jennie lived many of the biggest names in vaudeville. The proximity of these stars would contribute to Shemp, Moe, and Curly's tremendous drive to achieve success in show business.

The second event in '97 was the birth of Jennie's fourth son. On a warm day in June, Jennie stopped work long enough to get word to Mrs. Solomon, her midwife, that her labor had started in earnest, and Moses Horwitz pushed his way into the world on the morning of June 19, 1897, and—voila—Jennie's second Stooge was born.

Moe was sturdily built, with a slim, funny face surrounded by brownish-black hair. He had steel-blue eyes like his mother and weighed in at exactly eight pounds.

Jennie had plans through the years for this, her fourth son. At four, she was sure he'd be a dentist, at six a doctor, at seven a violinist, and at ten a lawyer. In later years, Moe would prove to be her fourth disappointment when, like Shemp, he would also become an actor and then a comedian, both of which were professions that were decidedly not Jennie's cup of tea.

The family was growing, and it was no easy job raising four sons, catering to a husband, and swinging major real estate deals. To increase the family's income and enable her to buy more property in the Bensonhurst area, Jennie rented out several rooms in the house to boarders. Desperate for household help, she arranged for Sol's fourteen-year-old sister, Esther, to come to America from Europe. Strong, robust, and willing, Esther was expected to care for the house, for Sol and the kids, and for a houseful of boarders. This was no easy task, especially with the wild and mischievous Moe and Shemp constantly underfoot.

Esther Horwitz Feldman (Jennie's indentured servant) with her daughter Emily, circa 1918.

Courtesy of Emily Trager

Bensonhurst Station, circa 1910–1920.   *Brooklyn Historical Society*

Bensonhurst, Brooklyn. View of east side of Thirteenth Avenue looking north from Eighty-Fifth Street, circa 1910.

Brooklyn Historical Society

Twenty-Second Avenue, the show street of Bensonhurst, circa 1910.   *Brooklyn Historical Society*

Esther was miserable. She had no room of her own and, on many nights, would curl up on the stairs in an effort to get some sleep. It was catch as catch can, since each rented room meant extra income for Jennie.

In desperation, the homesick young girl complained to her married sister, Celia, who was living in New York City.

As the story goes, on a dark night in 1901, Celia's husband, Barnet Marx, went to Jennie's house in Bath Beach and spirited young Esther away. The next day he put her on a train to St. Paul, where she would stay with her older sister.

When Jennie found out that Esther was gone, she was incensed. According to an agreement between Esther's parents in Lithuania and Jennie, the girl was required to work in the Horwitz home until she paid back the cost of her fare. Jennie accused Barnet of breaking the contract and kidnapping Esther. She brought the matter to court, but the case was promptly dropped, the judge's reason for his decision forever lost in obscurity.

Moe was four at the time of Esther's indenture and was never aware of this side of Jennie's character. In his eyes, his mother could do no wrong, and Moe's memories of her were all pleasant ones—with one exception: that loathsome time when his mother, who had always wanted a daughter, put his hair into curls. Poor Moe went through hell when he went to school, his funny, freckled face surrounded by large sausage-shaped curls. Naturally, the boys made fun of him, and it was a constant battle to keep his self-respect. This was a traumatic period for Moe and, throughout his life, the only unpleasant memory he ever had of his model mama.

As the years rolled by, Jennie's real estate business continued to thrive, and she divided her time between buying and selling land and working for charitable causes. Charity for Jennie was a second religion. She helped young couples who were thinking of divorce work out their problems and spent long hours at the Home for the Aged in Brooklyn, where she donated food, clothing, and money and was referred to by the residents as their guardian angel.

Jennie found time for everyone and everything. Surprisingly, she had terrific stamina for a chunky not-quite-five-footer. Her constant cry was "You get out of life what you put into it." And this remarkable young woman was putting her all into life while the Horwitz family was growing and prospering.

Sol and Jennie should have been happy and content—and maybe they were—but they rarely displayed any emotion.

Jennie's cousin, Emily Trager, said, "Jennie bugged Sol all the time, constantly reiterating the song title from *Fiddler on the Roof*. 'Do you love me?' was Jennie's constant cry to Sol."

And Sol must have heard Jennie's cry and acted on it, for on October 22, 1903, the same year that the Wright brothers successfully flew their plane at Kitty Hawk, the last of the Horwitz children was born in a hospital in Brooklyn. No midwife this time for Jennie. She was now a woman of means and had young Dr. Duffy, the brother of Moe's sixth-grade schoolteacher, deliver her new baby. Jennie was certain that the law of odds would be in her favor this time and she would finally give birth to the girl she had dreamed about.

Once again, for the fifth time, she was to be disappointed. Jerome Lester "Curly" Horwitz was all boy. It was only a temporary disappointment to Jennie but none at all to millions of fans yet unborn or, in later years, to Moe and Larry, whose success as the world-famous Three Stooges might never have been achieved with a chubby, bald-headed girl in their act.

Barnet Marx and Sol's oldest sister, Celia Horwitz, on her engagement day, 1893, when Celia was living with Sol and Jennie in America.

Courtesy of Stanley Marx

2

A BABY NAMED BABE (1903–1919)

Curly: Lover of Sports, Lover of Dance, and Just Plain Lover

Baby Curly, whom his brothers immediately nicknamed Babe, was a good child and no trouble for Jennie—that is, until his mischievous siblings, Moe and Shemp, showed him the ropes. Their wild, wacky, and inventive behavior reached dangerous proportions when, one day, Moe and Shemp took Curly's brand-new baby carriage, converted it into a "soapbox racer," and placed little Curly in it. When Jennie and Sol returned home and found their baby sitting happily astride this mad invention, perched atop a steep hill and poised for a downhill race, they almost blew their gaskets. Years later, Moe realized the danger of his boyhood prank and said, "It was a lucky thing we didn't kill him."

Despite numerous scoldings, Moe and Shemp continued their boyish pranks, with Curly always the "fall kid." On one windy, rainy night in 1908, Jennie and Sol left Moe and Shemp to care for five-year-old Curly. Our three little Stooges were soon ensconced on a seat in an upstairs bay window, with little Babe an eager, receptive audience as they prepared to blow wads of putty out the window with their peashooters. Within minutes, a man appeared on the street below, clutching his umbrella. Curly screamed with delight as Moe blew hard and a wad of putty splattered into the man's hand, the impact sending his umbrella into the air, where it tumbled away in the wind.

Curly's delight attracted the attention of his mischievous brothers, and there was no question in their minds who their next victim would be. It was a lucky break for little Curly that Jennie returned home early, just as dead-shot Moe was preparing to shoot a penny out from between her baby's fingers.

It is interesting to note that, as a child, Curly always took the brunt of his brothers' havoc, just as he would later on as a grown man during the making of his ninety-seven Three Stooges comedies.

Time was moving onward, and little Curly was developing into big Curly, getting taller and better looking with each passing day. As the youngest of the five Horwitz brothers, he was spoiled, but in spite of this, he was Moe's favorite, and my father became his second father, filling in for an ever-absent Sol. Moe took Curly to the beach regularly and taught him to swim and play the ukulele and tried his best to get him through school. Curly was a fair student, but unless Jennie, Sol, and Moe prodded him, he rarely attended his classes. All through his school years, Curly's first love and favorite pastime was playing hooky.

Unlike their kid brother, Moe and Shemp's favorite pastime in Bensonhurst was putting on plays at the homes of their friends. Curly would usually join the cast and even at this early age had trouble recalling his lines. Taking over as leader of the group as early as 1910, Moe solved Curly's memory problem and may have been the first inventor of cue cards. He would write Curly's cues on adhesive tape and stick the tape to his own forehead so brother Babe could read them.

In these neighborhood shows, Curly, at the age of seven, loved to prance about before an audience, egged on by the sound of applause. He was undisturbed by the fact that he was always cast as the female lead. A dab of paint on his cheeks, lipstick on his lips, and an old string mop plopped on his head with the fringe hanging down over his cute, round face, and there was Curly in drag at the ripe old age of seven.

In 1913 Curly spent a bit more time in school, but it wasn't the three *R*s—*r*eadin', *r*itin' and *r*ithmetic—he studied. Uh-uh, in Curly's case it was the two *B*s—*b*asket*b*all. He was a terrific player and the star of his school team. At the same time that Curly was addicted to laying up the ball on the school court, teenage Shemp and Moe were going to parties and entertaining their friends. Shemp had matured into a real Chaplinesque clown and would keep everyone in stitches with his wild stories, fast-paced jokes, and kooky antics, with Moe always playing the

Rear yard of a typical Bensonhurst house, circa 1910.   *Brooklyn Historical Society*

"straight boy." It was the favorable reactions of their young friends that encouraged the pair to turn professional, and Moe, always the leader, decided to prepare a blackface act for himself and Shemp in an attempt to break into vaudeville.

During the weeks that followed this momentous decision, the two brothers smeared their faces with burnt cork and practiced their corny old jokes, while little Curly, left out for the first time, looked on with envy, impatiently waiting for Shemp and Moe's opening night.

Poor Curly was forced to maintain his patience when his brothers' entry into show business was suddenly postponed indefinitely. Moe had gotten his first big break and took off for the entire summer. How could he turn down the opportunity to perform on the showboat *Sunflower* with Captain Billy Bryant? With Moe gone, Shemp was forced to find another partner, and Curly, watching and waiting, wished that it would be him. But such was not the case. He would have to wait many more years for the opportunity to cast his lot in with his talented brothers.

Moe returned from the Mississippi at summer's end and finally began his professional career in earnest, joining Shemp in their blackface act at the Mystic Theater on Fifty-Third Street near Third Avenue. The two aspiring performers leapt for joy as they signed a contract for the grandiose sum of thirty dollars a week and at last received their billing as "Howard and Howard."

On opening day, Shemp and Moe took Curly with them and sat him in the front row, where he waited excitedly for his brothers' debut. Once again, brother Babe was to be disappointed. Howard and Howard were last on the bill for a specific reason. The greedy theater manager knew how corny their act was, and to clear out the theater for new customers who were lined up outside, he dashed onstage and shouted, "Howard and Howard, up and at 'em!"

Moe and Shemp charged onto the stage and, just as the manager had planned, the audience left the theater en masse after their first two jokes.

It was a heartbreaking experience for the two, with their only solace the wild, exuberant applause of their brother, sitting alone in the empty theater.

Whether on the stage or in the audience, Curly loved the theater. In his mind his two brothers were superstars, and he was determined to emulate them.

Curly's oldest brother, Irving, at age 13 (1904).

It was 1914. Europe had gone to war, but in America the movies were on their way to becoming a national entertainment and vaudeville was flourishing. The Brooklyn neighbors of Moe, Shemp, and Curly Howard were such vaudeville headliners as Trixie Friganza; Adelaide and Hughes, a top-flight dance team; Charles Dale of the comedy team Smith and Dale; and Harry Fox, who worked with the Dolly Sisters. Added to this rarified environment (and just around the corner from where Curly lived) were the Grand Opera House and the Crescent and Montauk Theaters, where he watched plays whose titles alone quickened his pulse: *Ten Nights in a Barroom*, *The Two Orphans*, *Uncle Tom's Cabin*, and *Seven Keys to Baldpate*.

Curly longed desperately to be part of this wonderful world of show business, but he felt alone and left out at this point in his life. Moe and Shemp were finally succeeding with their act, mother Jennie was deeply involved in real estate deals and charitable causes that took up most of her time, and his father spent all day chanting the Torah at the local synagogue. It was a period in his life when he found himself marking time, waiting for that day when he would stand on the stage with the footlights shining in his eyes and the audience cheering his performance.

It was 1916 when, at age thirteen, Curly's first performance before an adult audience finally took place. He strode brazenly onto the stage at his father's shul to be bar mitzvahed.

Even this event in his show business life was a tough haul for Curly. School, and especially Hebrew school, was not one of his first loves, but for the son of Solomon it was a must, and Curly performed with all the spirit and punch that was later to make him a comedy genius.

Curly at age thirteen, around the time of his bar mitzvah (1916).

Several months after his bar mitzvah, Curly asked Shemp and Moe to go back with him to their Hebrew school at the Congregation Sons of Israel, their alma mater. All three were taught by Dr. Agat, a scholarly old man with very poor eyesight who moved about like an arthritic snail. Always looking for laughs, Curly, Moe, and Shemp decided to play one of their pranks on the old doctor. They snuck to the rear of the classroom and crouched under one of the long wooden benches. When old Dr. Agat entered, all three began raising the bench slowly up and down, like a Ouija board at a séance.

Overly superstitious, the old doctor, certain he was seeing an apparition, rushed off to the rabbi's study, screaming for him to come see what was happening. When the astute rabbi caught sight of the wooden bench seeming to hover in midair in the back of the room and heard muffled laughter, he caught on at once. Glaring at Dr. Agat, he whispered, "Doctor! Don't you know those devils yet? It's the Horwitz boys."

When these three delinquents arrived home, word of their prank had already reached Jennie, and all hell broke loose. Naturally, all of the dressing down was done by Jennie, the taskmaster, and not by Sol, who throughout his life would never lay a finger on his boys.

Curly (top left) at age fifteen with the members of the P.S. 128 basketball team (1918).

He was the bogeyman that Jennie created, a bogeyman that scared nobody. It is interesting to note that, in this era, catching hell was much more physical than it is today. According to my father, it was usually a hard smack across the face or upstairs and down with your pants, followed by several whacks on the bare buttocks with a strap used for sharpening razors. But Shemp, Moe, and Curly were the lucky ones. Their punishment, though severe, was mild by comparison to that of some of their friends. Other families, at the least display of disrespect from their kids, would crack them over the head with whatever was handy, be it a broom, rolling pin, or mop handle.

The three neophyte Stooges played their next prank against their older brother Jack, whose major goal in life was making money. This was something that Curly just couldn't understand. Jack was a saver and kept all his money hidden in a sock tied inside his pajama pants. One night, just before bedtime, young Curly noticed with envy the big bulge in his brother's crotch. Curious, he spied on him the next morning and discovered, with relief, that Jack's bulging whatsis was in fact his secret sock.

Zingo! Back he went to Moe and Shemp to spill the beans. Jack, a sound saver, was also a sound sleeper. The next night, Shemp, Moe, and Curly tiptoed into Jack's bedroom and picked him clean. Poor money-mad Jack went bananas for several days searching the entire house and wondering about the grins on his brothers' faces, until finally our wacky young Stooges returned his money.

Like most teenagers, Curly's prime interest in life soon turned to the fairer sex. To please the girls, he became a clotheshorse, dressing in the latest fashions of the day. By now, Jennie had consummated many big real estate deals and could afford to clothe Curly in a way she had never been able to do for her other sons. The cut of his jacket, his cap and tie, and the bouton-niere in his lapel were the best that money could buy, and week by week his wardrobe grew.

But Curly was never one to think of the future. In Bath Beach when the summer of 1916 came, it was time for fun and relaxation, and Curly would spend his days frolicking amidst sand and surf. Sol would, as always, grab his Jewish newspaper while Jennie would make her business contacts during walks with prospective buyers and sellers in Ulmer Park. The summer of 1916 was also the time that Jennie decided to stake Sol in a business of his own by fulfilling his dream of becoming a manufacturer of ladies' ready-to-wear. She investigated the potential of this business from all angles, found it sound, and proceeded to take the necessary steps to start Sol on his way. Having no time to help run the business, she finally acquiesced and left it to her husband to make it on his own.

Jennie was not a spendthrift, but when she started charging all of Curly's new clothes, Sol, who was closemouthed, finally raised hell. Jennie's answer was a sound one. She wanted to establish credit. If and when hard times came, every door would be open to her. And hard times soon would come, with the crash of the stock market and the start of the Great Depression of the 1930s.

Gravesend Bay in Bensonhurst, Curly's stomping grounds for swimming and fishing.
Brooklyn Historical Society

Sol bubbled over with confidence and, with full financing from the Horwitz coffers, charged ahead into the world of big business. He was owner, boss, and salesman and quickly found a Midwestern chain-store buyer who agreed to place an order for three thousand skirts. In Sol's mind, his fortune was made. Moe, who was working at Sol's factory for the summer, begged his father to look up the buyer in Dun & Bradstreet to be certain he was legitimate. Sol, who could only see good in everyone, responded with "Did you see the man's eyes? He's as honest as the day is long." Ever confident, Sol shipped the three thousand skirts and never saw a dime. Between this major error and the pricing of his skirts at four cents apiece instead of sixty-four cents, he was out of business within months.

Curly, meanwhile, was enjoying the summer, his favorite time of year. July 1916 was hot and muggy, and to escape the Brooklyn infestation of mosquitoes, Curly, who loved to swim, spent most of his time at the beach. Brother Moe, his mentor during these days, was employed on weekends as one of Bath Beach's assistant lifeguards, and Curly reveled in watching his big brother pull hapless victims from the surf. Throughout his life, Curly never forgot and often related stories about Moe's heroism as a lifeguard and how Moe and three of his friends eventually joined an act with the Annette Kellerman Diving Girls, which consisted of ten shapely young swimmers. Actually, there were only six Kellerman girls, as Moe and his three friends, dressed as girls, formed the remainder of the troupe. Curly watched enthralled as the "girls," including Moe, took turns doing thirty-foot dives into a tank seven feet long, seven feet wide, and seven feet deep. Moe and his buddies dove into the water wearing long one-piece bathing suits, caps on their heads, and balls of crumpled newspaper stuffed inside their suits to augment their concave bosoms. After each dive, Curly, who stood tankside, would crack up as the paper falsies dropped down around the boys' stomachs and they would have to struggle underwater, gyrating comically, trying to push their bosoms back up where they belonged before they emerged to take their bows.

Later in the season, Moe quit Miss Kellerman's troupe after one of the female divers misjudged the tank and was killed.

For Curly the beach was not only a place to swim but a place to girl watch. He delighted in staring at their cute little bodies in their tight little jerseys, which clung quite pleasingly when they were wet.

This youngest of the Horwitzes was "beach smart" and had a clever method for attracting the attention of the girls. Perched high atop the railing of the pier, at least fifteen feet above the water, he would dive off into about three feet of sparkling white foam. The girls would scream, then *ooo* and *aaah*, gathering around Curly, waiting for him to break his neck. When he didn't, they'd throw their arms around him and congratulate him. He never tired of those hugs and repeated his trick over and over again.

Besides girls and swimming, another love during his teens that definitely affected him in later life was food. Curly ate anything and everything: from his mother's gefilte fish to those hot, charred potatoes dumped in beach bonfires and given the Irish name "Mickeys." Life in

Curly, second from left, and members of the "Bath Beach Gang," according to Curly's girlfriend Ernestine Boehm Goldman, who took this photograph at Captain's Pier.

Courtesy of Ernestine Boehm Goldman

those heady days was sweet for Curly: strumming his ukulele, plunking out the strains of "Oh, You Beautiful Doll," eyeing shapely, tanned female bodies in tight bathing suits, and sinking his teeth into charred and blackened fluffy baked potatoes.

Toward summer's end, Curly gave up his beach bumming and joined Moe and Shemp on their train ride to the Horwitz farm in Chatham, New York. This 116-acre parcel of land 150 miles from New York City was Jennie's latest real estate purchase. She not only wanted it for a business investment but felt it would be a healthy place for her sons to spend their summers, away from the heat of the city and far away from that monkey business—show business.

Moe, unbeknownst to his mother, would sandwich in his vaudeville stints with Shemp between his trips to Chatham while his older brother Jack and a professional farmer worked on the farm full-time.

Curly, an animal lover, was fascinated by anything with four legs. On his first trip to the new farm, he took a special liking to a big, fat, curly-tailed pig. This un-kosher beast came with the property, and as soon as Jennie discovered it romping with Curly, she lost no time in selling it, at a discount price, to a neighboring farmer.

Although at home Curly would shirk all forms of housework, on the farm he pitched in with the chores and learned everything from running the cream separator to churning butter and tending the truck garden. Every farm animal became his friend, and he awoke each morning at four thirty to feed them.

Shemp, on the other hand, hated farm work and would rather goof off. He never tired of running around the Horwitz spread in the maddest-looking outfit, which consisted of bright red flannel underwear, an old Continental Army coat, and an early American military hat. Each day would find him playing his favorite practical joke. He would don his kooky costume, strike a comical pose in the middle of a cornfield, and wait for the neighboring farmers to pass by and stare in amazement at what they thought was one strange-looking scarecrow. Of all his big brothers' many pranks, this one delighted Curly the most.

Another of Shemp and Moe's capers that Curly loved was watching as his brothers shaved off only one side of their bushy brown beards and then following along as they marched through town. Seeing the expressions on the shocked faces of the staid townspeople never failed to crack up Curly, no matter how many times he witnessed it.

Later that summer, the boys received a letter from Jennie stating that she was coming to the farm for the weekend and wanted them to pick her up at the Chatham Railroad Station. This time, Shemp and Moe decided to try one of their pranks on their own mother. Curly, knowing Jennie's stodgy, old-fashioned ways, warned his brothers that she wouldn't appreciate

Moe, left, a friend, and Shemp in costume on the Chatham Farm (1916).

The Chatham Farm. Jack Horwitz (right) aboard a hay wagon with his fellow farmers (1916).

Shemp and Irving's wife, Nettie, on the Chatham farm in 1916.   *Courtesy of Margie Golden*

The Horwitzes' Chatham farm. Left to right: Curly; Moe; Curly's dog, King; Jennie; and Sol's sister Celia (1916).

Nettie and Irving on the farm. He is wearing what every well-dressed farmer should wear (1918).

Courtesy of Margie Golden

Jennie and her boys (left to right) Shemp, Jack, Irving, and Moe.

their crazy monkeyshines. His warning went unheeded. There was too much theater in Shemp and Moe, and once these two clowns decided to put on their act, there was no stopping them.

As always, Curly was beside himself with excitement and had difficulty holding back his laughter at the ludicrous appearance of his two crazily costumed brothers as they rode into town on the farm's "surrey with the fringe on top" to pick up their mother.

When Jennie arrived at the railroad station, she glanced casually at what she was certain were two maniacs standing near the station platform, dressed in red flannels and Continental Army coats with silly-looking black tricornes on their heads. Their half-beards added a final touch of insanity as they stood stiffly by the surrey, each holding a horse by the bridle. There was absolutely no sign of recognition on Jennie's face as she searched about for her sons. Finally, she heard Curly's giggles from behind the surrey and realized that these two maniacs were Shemp and Moe. To say that she was shocked would be an understatement. She cringed with embarrassment, her discomfort increasing by the minute as curious townspeople gathered around them, staring and laughing at her two offspring. Livid, she hissed under her breath to Moe and Shemp, "How can you do such insane things—you meshuganas."

But life on the farm wasn't all fun and games in the summer of 1916. There were mishaps, the first of which occurred when Curly cut through a nest of yellow jackets while mowing a field. Moe was nearby, and both had to race to the nearest stream and dive in, with the swarm of angry insects in hot pursuit. It was a real-life forerunner of many Stooges antics as they limped back to the farm, soaking wet and covered with masses of swollen red lumps.

Annoying, yes, but a minor mishap when compared to the most traumatic event of this particular summer. It is paradoxical that throughout Curly's life, as much as he loved animals, he also liked to hunt. One of his prized possessions was his .22-caliber rifle. Unfortunately, it had a hair trigger. While relaxing, Curly placed his gun on his lap, barrel down, between his crossed legs, unaware that the muzzle was resting against the side of his foot. His fingers inadvertently pressed against the trigger. A loud *crack* rang out and the bullet discharged, shattering the bone in his ankle.

It is a scientific fact that no pain is felt at the instant one receives a gunshot wound. Curly's pain would come moments later and, although intermittent, would last a lifetime.

Panicked, his friend dragged him home, where an ashen-faced Moe helped his kid brother into bed. Shock had set in, and Curly lay like a corpse, blood pouring from his foot.

Brother Irving in 1912, in real estate with Jennie.

Jennie, at right, in Bath Beach with one of her sisters. Note ROOM TO LET sign in the background.

Moe, terribly rattled by the sight of all that blood, wrapped Curly's foot in a towel, carried him into the farm's surrey, and drove like a maniac to the nearest hospital in Albany, New York.

At the hospital, it was touch and go as to whether Curly would lose his foot. Luck was with him. His foot would not have to be amputated. The doctor recommended immediate surgery that would entail deliberately breaking his ankle bone and then putting his entire foot in a cast until the bones knitted properly. Curly had never been in a hospital before and panicked at the thought of an operation. He instantly rejected the doctor's recommendation and insisted that the wound be allowed to heal by itself.

Family, friends, and fans would speculate for years to come as to whether Curly made the right choice that night in Albany. The wound did heal by itself without surgery, but the residual effects would leave him with a limp for the rest of his life and would cause him pain if he was on his feet for extended periods of time. But Curly was a trouper and never allowed his handicap to interfere with either his work or his play.

The traumatic summer of 1916 passed and was followed by an uneventful fall and winter. Then, in the spring of 1917, the United States declared war on Germany. Curly was fourteen at the time, struggling to graduate from grammar school, while Moe and Shemp were performing their comedy act for both the Loews and Keith circuits.

Working for two vaudeville circuits at the same time was a major no-no, as there was an unwritten agreement between the circuits that if you worked for one, the other would not hire you. Shemp and Moe, ever the inventive pranksters, got around this no-no by disguising themselves with the aid of makeup and performed a blackface act for Keith and, under another name, a whiteface act for Loews. They got away with this trick for months, until Shemp's number was called and he was drafted into the army. Moe found himself unemployed—but not for long. Shemp was discharged after only a few months of service when the army discovered he was a bed wetter. Always a sensitive young man, and a lifelong scaredy-cat, Shemp was terrified by the thought of soldiering in a shooting war and was greatly relieved when Uncle Sam rejected him. Throughout his life he thanked God for supplying him with a weak bladder.

While the Horwitz family was celebrating Shemp's safe return from the wars, Jennie, ever the astute real estate businesswoman, received an offer for the Chatham farm that she couldn't refuse. But, as always, her children came first, and especially her baby Curly. The escrow stipulated that the new owner could not take occupancy until the fall of 1918, allowing Curly one extra summer on the farm with the animals he loved.

The summer of 1918 found Curly enjoying life by helping with the harvesting of the wheat, corn, and buckwheat crops, and especially loving every minute of tending the farm's animals. Moe and Shemp were also there for this last summer, and they were later joined by their other brother, Jack, who married his boyhood sweetheart, Laura Brukoff, and spent his honeymoon on the farm. Jack later moved to Laura's hometown of Pittsburgh, where he eventually got a job with the Metropolitan Life Insurance Company and rose to district manager. Jack would never be an actor, and his only link to show business would be selling bundles of life insurance to his three famous brothers, Moe, Shemp, and Curly.

Shemp, returned from the war (1917).

When the war ended in November, life was running smoothly for the Horwitzes. Jennie's real estate business was booming while Sol was happy and serene, spending most of his time in prayer and, thanks to Jennie's empathy, made to feel as though he were part of her success. Irving, the oldest of the Horwitz offspring, was twenty-nine, happily married, and a successful insurance man like his younger brother Jack. Shemp and Moe were back in show business, moving up the entertainment industry ladder in two circuits with their black- and whiteface acts, and Curly, now sixteen, had crossed over the threshold from boyhood to manhood.

All through my research on Curly's boyhood, I was dying to find someone who actually went to school with him. I knew, without a doubt, that someone was out there somewhere, but I was aware that the odds of my finding him or her was like finding a needle in a haystack.

Then on April 13, 1985, my husband received a letter from an Ernestine Goldman, who mentioned that she had seen some publicity about a new movie on the Stooges that Norman had proposed, and this had given her the impetus to write to him. The next line in the letter jumped out at us. It read, "The mention of the Stooges brought back fond memories of Jerome (Curly). We went to school together when he was one of the Horwitz boys."

Need I say I was ecstatic? It took over a week to get in touch with Ernestine, as she had gone to the hospital for tests. When she finally answered my phone call, I was surprised to hear the lovely voice of a youthful, sharp eighty-year-old. Here is what she had to say:

The Marguerite Bryant Players stock company (1919), Oakford Park, Pennsylvania.
Moe, second from left; Shemp, second from right.

Moe and Shemp about to start their careers in vaudeville, July 19, 1919.

Shemp and Moe onstage during their act as "Howard and Howard" (1919).

INTERVIEW

Courtesy of the subject

Ernestine Boehm Goldman

April 19, 1985

JOAN: So you knew Curly and his brothers between 1916 and 1919?

ERNESTINE: I was more friends with Curly than the other brothers. They were older. Curly's name wasn't Curly in school, it was Babe.

JOAN: Do you mind telling me what year you were born?

ERNESTINE: 1906.

JOAN: And your maiden name?

ERNESTINE: Boehm. My name was Ernestine Boehm, but everyone called me Ernie.

JOAN: What street did you live on in Bensonhurst?

ERNESTINE: Eighty-Fifth Street off of Eighteenth Avenue. I was at 1827, and Curly lived on the same block—a few houses down.

JOAN: Then Curly was going to school in Bensonhurst?

ERNESTINE: Yes, that's right. P.S. 128.

JOAN: You were born in 1906—that would make you how old when you knew Curly?

ERNESTINE: I must have been about—oh, maybe fourteen, fifteen, sixteen. Babe would come over with the boys, play ball, and wait for me. They would come over on Sunday. I was working at a real estate company. They used to come over to my house, too, where I lived with an aunt of mine. And years later—I recall—when I got married. It was about a week before my wedding. My husband [to be] and I were walking on Eighty-Fifth Street, and all of a sudden we see him [Curly] coming down the stairs of our apartment house. We asked him where he was coming from, and he said, "I'm here for your wedding." And we said, "We're not going to be married until next week."

JOAN: [Laughing.] What else do you remember about Curly?

ERNESTINE: What can I tell you? We used to play together. I recall him sitting on the running board of the cars, playing his ukulele.

JOAN: How long did you go to school with Curly?

ERNESTINE: I went to school with Babe mostly in the later grades [of public school].

JOAN: Did Curly graduate?

ERNESTINE: He sure did—that I know—yes.

JOAN: Did he go on to high school?

ERNESTINE: That I don't know. We saw a lot of each other in the early years, and after that we didn't.

JOAN: What were his parents like—that is, if you knew them?

ERNESTINE: They were real elderly parents [when Curly was sixteen Jennie was fifty] and very religious.

JOAN: She was said to be very stern and very efficient.

ERNESTINE: Oh, yes. She had the upper hand.

JOAN: When you knew Curly, did his parents spend time with him?

ERNESTINE: He was on his own mostly.

JOAN: What was Curly really like?

ERNESTINE: Full of the devil. Full of the devil but a nice guy. I remember going to the movies with him once—with some friends—and he put his arm around my shoulder, and all of a sudden his hand went down a little bit. I took his hand and I threw it off, and I walked out of the movies and he followed me.

JOAN: How old was he then?

ERNESTINE: About sixteen.

JOAN: He became quite a womanizer. He was married four times.

ERNESTINE: Oh my God. Really? Oh, I'm glad I didn't marry him! Oh my goodness!

JOAN: He had two children with two different wives.

ERNESTINE: Babe? Oh, you're telling me something I never knew.

JOAN: You're going to be fascinated by this book. [Pause.] He was said to have been good at sports—was it basketball?

ERNESTINE: Yes. And baseball, too.

JOAN: Would you say he was a happy kid?

ERNESTINE: Oh, yes.

JOAN: Was he close to his brothers?

ERNESTINE: Yes, but they were busy all the time.

JOAN: Now, if you look back at young Curly, what stands out in your mind?

ERNESTINE: I . . . don't know. . . . I just liked him. Yes—I put up with him. [Pause.] He lived right on the block. It was bu-dee-ful.

I was really excited when I hung up. I felt as though I had been able to go back through the years and get an honest glimpse—even though a small one—of Curly the teenager from a woman's point of view.

And Ernestine's words, "I just liked him," when I asked her what stood out in her mind about Curly made me realize that even in the early days, Curly must have had that special charm.

And Curly had plenty of charm as he matured into a good-looking, curly-haired young man. He was out of school, and having no professional skills, his dream was to follow in the footsteps of his two successful brothers. Knowing his mother's disdain for the acting profession and her constant aggravation over two of her sons frolicking about as thespians, he fought his desires and once again turned all his energies to the girls. Using skills that were honed by his brother Moe when the two played their ukuleles and harmonized together on the beach, Curly turned every ounce of his creativity to the fairer sex, singing and dancing his days and nights away as an endless stream of pretty young damsels clung to the arm of this cute, talented young guy from Bath Beach.

Curly's innocent, happy teens were about to segue into his twenties. Respecting his mother's wishes, happy-go-lucky Curly shelved his show business aspirations, never dreaming that one day he would become world famous, coining such catch phrases as "n'yuk-n'yuk" and "why soitenly," or that decades after his untimely death he would become a cult hero to millions of devoted fans who would imitate his every mannerism.

But this was still 1919, and as the teens on the calendar also drew to a close, Curly was moving closer to the Roaring Twenties, which would rumble with thunderous applause for Shemp and Moe but bring the Great Depression to the Horwitz family as well as to America and the rest of the world.

3

THE '20s

Curly Roars Through the '20s • Marriage #1 • A Trip to Paris • The Start of a Career

Without a doubt, the major event in Curly's life during the '20s was his first marriage, the union between Curly and his mysterious bride that for decades was a mystery to my family and me. Now, thanks to the research required for this book, it is finally becoming somewhat less obscure.

I don't recall when I first heard that my uncle had married in his youth and that my grandmother had broken up the marriage shortly after the wedding. I was probably in my teens and never really paid much attention to this bit of family gossip. The one thought that stuck in my head at that time was that if Jennie was able to make her son leave his bride after several months of married life, then Curly must have been very young.

Not until I was researching for my first book, in 1981, did I attempt to locate Curly's marriage license, hoping to find out the mystery girl's name. I spent a lot of money and came up empty-handed. Today, I am still not certain what her name was, but I have a bit more information about her that I pieced together after questioning members of my family.* After extensive interviews, some of which were with distant relations whom I had never even met, I came up with a few more brushstrokes in my attempt to clarify a very fuzzy portion of the canvas of Curly's life.

My presumption that Curly's mother instigated the divorce because her son was too young appears to be wrong. I was floored when I discovered that Curly actually married his first wife when he was in his midtwenties.

Although Jennie still had Curly completely under her thumb in the early '20s, he saw very little of her or his brothers Shemp and Moe during that period. Jennie, in 1922, was fully occupied with her real estate business, and Shemp and Moe were on the road, appearing in vaudeville theaters across the country.

During their absence, Curly lived for letters from Moe, who always kept in touch, sometimes phoning and telling his kid brother the details of the exciting things that were taking place in his career. News that Moe had met his old friend, Ted Healy, at the Prospect Theater in Brooklyn and that he and Shemp had been asked to join Ted in his vaudeville act gave Curly mixed feelings. Although he was thrilled about this big break in his brothers' careers, he also had pangs of envy about not being a part of their show business success. Life was dull for Curly in 1922. His mother had made plans for him to go back to school and learn a trade, but Curly had absolutely no interest in soldering pipes or connecting wires, which were far cries from his dream of being on the stage, singing, dancing, acting, and feeling the exhilaration that came with the thunder of applause that he was certain he would get one day.

The years crept by at a snail's pace, as if time were passing by in slow motion. In 1924 Curly was twenty-one and, although no longer a minor, was still suffering from the pressures brought about by a domineering mother who still considered him her baby. He didn't feel like a man, and although his mother's domination was beginning to get to him, he was incapable of breaking away and upsetting her.

In the winter of 1924, Curly's beloved beach was too cold, and he would have to wait until summer to find any diversion there. To fill his empty days and pass the time, he would polish his parents' Hupmobile over and over. He envied his friend Lester Friedman, who was a bookworm and could bury himself in a novel and never come out, but reading for Curly had always been a chore, and as much as he tried, he could not find an escape in literature.

Curly spent those long winter days looking forward to the nights. Night was when he came alive. He was an excellent dancer, and evenings usually found him at Brooklyn's famous Triangle Ballroom, his favorite nightspot. Spectators would often stare in admiration at his lightness of foot and wonderful sense of rhythm, and although this was a far cry from his dreams of the stage, at least it helped suppress his hidden desires.

---

* Years after the first edition of this biography was published, the marriage license finally surfaced. For the story of its discovery and updated details on Curly's first marriage and the timeline of his early adulthood, see the afterword, page 181.

I tried to picture him in his favorite haunt. I let my imagination take over, and in my mind I could almost see the crowded dance hall, with its flashing lights, and hear the '20s music. Curly is there, handsome, twenty-one years old with wavy chestnut-brown hair, gliding gracefully across the dance floor. He is dressed to kill in the latest fashion, and there is a pretty girl in his arms, wearing a very short dress with the tops of her stockings rolled neatly just below the hemline. Could this be the mystery girl whom Curly would marry one day? The secret still remained hidden. Ted Gell, an usher at Moe's wedding, described her as "in her late twenties, attractive, and definitely not Jewish." My cousin Bernice, on the other hand, described her as "definitely Jewish, a cute little thing with her hair bobbed and wearing a short dress of the period." Another cousin, Emily Trager, said, "She was an older woman, a friend of Jennie's."

Among the diversity of descriptions, I am certain of only one fact: she was definitely pretty, since throughout his life, Curly's taste always ran to attractive women.

I thought about the many descriptions of Curly's first wife, and they brought me back to my reveries and to one of those many nights that he spent at the Triangle Ballroom. George Raft was a Triangle regular, and one wonders if he was there that night, watching Curly hold his pretty partner and expertly maneuver her through the steps of the Charleston. Did Curly lean over and croon the latest ballad of the day softly into her ear? Did he suddenly stop dancing and stare into her eyes with thoughts in his mind of running away with her, away from Jennie's control?

Curly's parents, Sol and Jennie, in 1929. A photo that Curly cut out and mounted on wood.

For a brief moment I was there with my uncle, watching, and then I snapped out of my fantasies and realized that I'd give my eyeteeth to interview this young lady—even though she would be in her eighties.

I stopped and shook myself out of dreamland. Thoughts raced through my mind. How could this young man in his twenties, with the girl of his dreams in his arms, have had to live his life according to the dictates of his mother? Then I recalled my cousin Dolly Sallin's words: "Jennie, on the one hand, had a sweet way about her, but when she would say, 'This is what you do,' *that* is what you did. She ruled her family [and especially Curly] with an iron hand." Dolly continued, "God! It took so many years for each son to transfer their love and decision making to their wives. Even my father [Jack] had problems. In an argument between Jennie and my mother, he would always take Jennie's side. It took years for him to cut the cord."

After Dolly's words, I fully realized that poor Curly was Jennie's "baby," and it must have been next to impossible for him to escape the clutches of my grandmother's iron hand.

In the summer of 1924, when Jennie finally discovered that Curly was going out regularly with one particular girl and spending a great deal of time dancing the night away at the Triangle Ballroom, she decided to spirit him away from Brooklyn, insisting that he join her and Sol on their annual trip to the mountains.

In July mother, father, and son left in the family Hupmobile for Saratoga Springs, an exclusive resort in upstate New York. Jennie and Sol were addicts for the waters of Saratoga, which were touted as wonderful for the skin as well as having superlative laxative powers. To them their yearly trip to Saratoga was a must for both its internal and external cleansing properties.

After several days of drinking the purifying waters and watching with boredom as the elderly doddered about through the park-like grounds heading for restrooms, poor Curly began to feel that he was living a nightmare. There was nothing for a young man of twenty-one to do at Saratoga: no ocean, no dancing, no sports—just an army of old people and a hot, smelly pool of mineral water. To make matters worse for frustrated Curly, there was Jennie, constantly nagging him to drink the water. "Drink, drink," Jennie would say. And, to shut her up, Curly drank.

Saratoga water was powerful stuff, and after several days at the resort, Curly discovered that its cathartic effect worked like a combination of dynamite and Milk of Magnesia, which forced him to carry a briefcase filled to the rim with toilet paper.

One day, Jennie, Sol, and Curly stopped at a bench to rest, when suddenly the volatile effects of the water hit Curly. He grabbed for his briefcase and raced wildly to the nearest restroom. Moments later, he exited, then stopped dead in his tracks. There was no beach in Saratoga Springs, no dance bands, but there was one adorable young lady chatting with Jennie and Sol.

Far from shy, Curly rushed up to them and introduced himself. After several minutes of conversation, he noticed the girl grinning from ear to ear and then slapping her hand to her mouth to choke back her laughter. Poor Curly looked down, and suddenly his cheeks turned red with embarrassment. Trailing out from his briefcase and back in the direction of the rest-

Curly's mother, real estate tycoon Jennie Horwitz,
on her annual visit to Saratoga Springs—where
Curly ran into big problems (1924).

room were several yards of snow-white toilet paper. With the regal nonchalance of a king pick-
ing up his train, Curly reeled in the toilet paper and, without missing a beat, tucked it neatly
back into the briefcase. The girl, impressed with his pantomime, could do nothing but say yes
when he asked her for a date.

Upon his return to Brooklyn at summer's end, Curly found a letter from Moe, and his face
lit up as he read:

Dear Babe,

Being on the road with Ted and Shemp is hectic; but life is treating me well. I have great news.
I met a lovely, young lady on the beach last year. Maybe you remember her, Helen Schonberger.
She was the one with the great legs. She walked over to us when we were playing the ukulele
on the beach—cute, short, dark hair and I'm going to marry her. We have set a date for the
wedding, June 7th. I'll call when I get back to give you more details.

Your loving brother,
Moe

Moe, relaxing between vaudeville performances at Brackenridge Park in San Antonio, Texas (1924).

Helen Howard, Curly's future sister-in-law (1923).

Although elated at the news, Curly couldn't quite recall a Helen. He searched his mind, trying to remember her, but there had been so many pretty, cute, short, dark-haired girls with great legs during those wonderful beach days with Moe that he just couldn't place her.

Moe and Helen's wedding was held on June 7, 1925, at the temple Congregation Sons of Israel—that same temple where the Horwitz boys had raised so much hell. Moe had ten ushers in attendance, and four of them were his brothers. He didn't want to hurt anyone's feelings, so there was no best man.

That same year, Curly received another bit of good news: his brother Shemp was also getting married—to a girl he knew from the neighborhood, Gertrude "Babe" Frank, the daughter of Jennie's favorite Bensonhurst builder.

Curly was now alone, the only bachelor among the five brothers. Then, in 1926, Moe abandoned show business and

Helen on her wedding day, in full regalia (1925).

Moe and Helen on their honeymoon (1925).

returned to Brooklyn with his bride, renting an apartment on Avenue J near Coney Island Avenue. My mother, Helen, was pregnant, and my father had dropped out of the act because touring with Ted Healy and Shemp took him away from his new wife for long periods of time.

In Brooklyn, with Jennie's help, Moe went into the real estate business. He bought several pieces of property in Bensonhurst and hired some of his old classmates as subcontractors to build several homes on speculation. Curly pitched in, hauling lumber and doing odd jobs, enjoying having something to fill his days. Upon completion of the houses, Moe discovered that he had built them too well. They were just too expensive for this Brooklyn neighborhood, and he found them next to impossible to sell without losing his shirt.

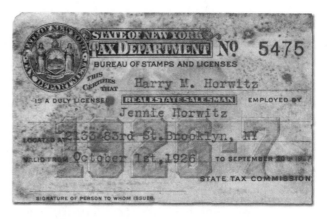

Moe abandons showbiz to be with his new wife, and Jennie helps Harry (a.k.a. Moe) to get his start in real estate.

Helen and Ted Healy meet for the first time, in 1927, after Moe failed at real estate and rejoined Healy's act.

On April 2, 1927, Moe's first child—the author—was born, and Curly was the first to see the new baby. His visit that day had a dual purpose: First, to play uncle to his new little niece, and second, to cheer up Moe, who had called that morning to inform him that the bank had taken over his unsold houses and he would have to file for bankruptcy.

In the months that followed, Curly's visits to Moe's apartment increased in frequency. He enjoyed seeing his brother and his wife and holding his new little niece in his arms. Later, in 1929, envying Moe's domestic life, he made his first major decision in life and, on impulse, without consulting his mother, rushed to a justice of the peace and married his mystery woman.

Things went well for several months, until circumstances forced Curly to tell his mother about his secret marriage. He had found out the hard way that two could not live as cheaply as one and was forced to come to her for a loan. When Jennie heard the news, she raved and ranted, shouting at Curly that she would support *him* but not his wife. As the weeks progressed, Jennie barely tolerated her newest daughter-in-law. Then, determined never to borrow from his mother again, Curly got his first job in show business. Although it was only part-time, he was hired to be guest comedic conductor for Orville Knapp's band.

One can imagine Jennie's reaction as she watched her son on the podium in front of the orchestra, his back to the audience, dressed in a swallowtail coat, its exaggerated black tails dragging across the stage floor. Then, as Curly moved his arms gracefully and waved his baton, the coat, which was made to self-destruct, ripped in half down the back. A few more waves of the baton and his pants split in two, and there stood Jennie's Curly, conducting the band in long underwear whose drop seat was held up by a giant safety pin. The band gave out with a dramatic drum roll, cymbals crashed, and amidst a roar of laughter, Curly took his bow, pants still draped around his ankles. As he comically hobbled off the stage, he glanced back to see what effect his routine had had on his mother—and there was Jennie, her expressionless, scowling face frozen like the head of the Sphinx.

Two weeks later, when Curly emerged from the family's traditional Friday-night dinner, his face was ashen. The actual words that were spoken that evening at the Horwitz house will forever remain a mystery. What is known is that Jennie had somehow convinced Curly to divorce his new wife.

Jennie must have felt some remorse for the trauma she had forced upon her son, for she invited Curly to join Sol and her on an extended European vacation. She would be visiting her old hometown in Lithuania and agreed to let Curly spend several weeks on his own in Paris. Always one for a bargain, Jennie was actually killing two birds with one stone. She was hopeful that in Paris Curly would forget about both of his loves—his ex-wife and the stage.

Curly, flanked by his mother and father, aboard the ship on his way to gay Paree (1929).

Curly's days in France were filled with fun and games. Pretty girls were everywhere, and not always the nicest girls. And Curly was getting an education that Jennie would neither have dreamed of nor approved of.

Paris was also a theatergoer's delight, with world-famous nightspots such as the Moulin Rouge and the Lido, which were filled with wonderful music and beautiful French girls. Brooklyn was never like this, and Curly reveled in the Parisian nightlife. Paris fashions intrigued him, and his mustache, which was on the bushy side when he left the States, was clipped and waxed at an elegant Left Bank salon.

During his stay in Europe, Curly had time to reflect upon the state of his life. With one marriage under his belt and a taste of world travel, there would be no holding him down. Jennie did not know it yet, but she had lost him. She would always have her son's love and respect, but from Paris on, he would be his own man—at least until he joined Moe in 1932, and then Moe would take charge.

On his return from Europe, Curly rejoined Orville Knapp's band. It was 1929, and Moe, after losing more than twenty thousand dollars in his real estate endeavors, was back in show business. He and Shemp were starring on Broadway with Ted Healy in *A Night in Venice*. Curly hated working in Knapp's band and was champing at the bit to quit and join Moe and Shemp. He was making a pittance as a comedic conductor and, never able to hold on to his money, constantly had to go to his mother for help.

Helen with daughter Joan and Ted Healy on his Darien, Connecticut, estate during rehearsals for *A Night in Venice* (1929).

Although Jennie had her faults, she was always generous when it came to her baby. Occasionally, at the Horwitzes' traditional Friday-night dinner, she would put a hundred-dollar bill under the dinner plates of each of her boys so that she could help Curly without making him feel as though he were the only failure among the five brothers.

One day, with one of those hundred-dollar bills burning a hole in his pocket, Curly decided to spend a week at his brother Jack's home in Pittsburgh. He went on a shopping spree and loaded up with gifts for Jack's wife, Laura, and their three kids, Rhea, Bernice, and Norman.

Curious, and wanting more details about Curly's visit to his brother Jack's home and other details about his life in the '20s, I telephoned my cousin Bernice Herzog for an interview on the subject.

Bernice, who was present during Curly's Pittsburgh visit, is the daughter of Curly's older brother, Benjamin "Jack" Horwitz, and Laura Brukoff. She was born in Pittsburgh, Pennsylvania, in 1919, graduated from Pennsylvania State College of Optometry, and had been practicing her profession in the Pittsburgh area for over forty years. She was married to Dr. Marvin Herzog, also an optometrist. The Herzogs had two grown children, Lynne and Jeff.

INTERVIEW

Courtesy of the subject

Bernice Herzog

January 1984

JOAN: Do you recall anything about Curly in the early days?

BERNICE: Uncle Babe [Curly] lived with us for a while in the late '20s. He was very fond of my mother—either because she and dad married on his birthday or because my mother and Jennie battled over real estate deals and my mom usually won.

JOAN: How did Jennie feel in those days about Moe and Shemp being in show business?

BERNICE: Jennie thought she was being cursed because her two boys were on the stage and her "baby" was straining at the bit to join them. In fact, to get Uncle Babe away from the theater, she sent him to Europe—I think he spent most of his time in Paris. When he returned, he was even more handsome than before, with his dark, wavy hair and very French waxed mustache. This is the time he came to Pittsburgh.

JOAN: Can you recall any funny stories related to Curly's visit?

BERNICE: Yes, one comes to mind. Jennie had two married sisters in Pittsburgh. One had thirteen children, the other six, so Curly had plenty of cousins who were his contemporaries to horse around with. I recall it was New Year's Eve and Curly and his cousins had gone to a party. When I came downstairs the next morning I found Uncle Babe sleeping in a chair. When I saw his face, I almost screamed in shock. One side of his upper lip was shaved down to the skin, leaving only half of his wonderful waxed mustache. When he awoke, he had no recollection of the prank that had been played on him, but he was a good sport and laughed and laughed.

JOAN: What did Curly do to keep busy? After all, he was out of school.

BERNICE: At this time in his life Babe was dying to be in the public eye, like his brothers, so he spent a lot of time in the Jewish restaurants doing what he did best—eating. One day when he was clowning around, telling jokes and singing, Joe Hiller saw him. Hiller, the owner of a large music store, hired Curly then and there to plug his songs. Curly loved to sing, and I recall he would go into Hiller's store, grab a piece of sheet music, and really stop traffic.

JOAN: Do you know anything about Curly's first wife—the mystery woman who married him in the late '20s?

BERNICE: I saw Babe's first wife on a visit to New York. She was a cute, short little thing with a real '20s hairdo. You know, with short sides and bangs—a real flapper type. Shortly

Curly clowns around with an unidentified elder. *Courtesy of Dr. Bernice Horwitz Herzog*

Curly with a full head of hair on his Pittsburgh visit in 1929, with cousins: Norman on his shoulders; Bernice, front left; Dolly, rear left; Margie, rear right; and Ruth, front right.

Courtesy of Dr. Bernice Horwitz Herzog

after this meeting, my family went back to Pittsburgh, and I heard them talking about the "annulment." As I recall, Curly and this first wife were together for only a short time—maybe a month. Grandma was pretty influential, and although she always claimed she had his marriage annulled, I think he was divorced and Jennie was ashamed to let anyone know. In those days, among orthodox Jews, a divorce was a disgrace.

JOAN: I heard from one of the ushers at Moe's wedding [Ted Gell] that the girl may have been Gentile. I heard from my cousin Emily that she was a much older woman and a friend of Jennie's.

BERNICE: As far as my recollections go, the girl was Jewish. I did hear that she was older, but Jennie wasn't mad about anything other than the fact she was going to lose him. Grandma broke that up, and she also had something to do with Babe and Elaine breaking up. I think Elaine's mother and [our] grandma got together. They both butted in too much.

JOAN: So Jennie was a tough woman and a meddler?

BERNICE: Oh, very much so.

JOAN: Can you tell me more about Jennie?

BERNICE: Jennie was vicious when it came to her real estate business. She and my mother were constantly at odds and in competition regarding their business deals, and my father [Jack] was in the middle. Jennie was strange. She just didn't want to let her children go, and even though my dad was married, he had to visit his mother every morning at breakfast time and again at dinner time. It was crazy. First, he ate breakfast at our house, then breakfast with his mother. Then he would stop off at Jennie's for dinner before going home to eat dinner at his own house. Very often my dad, in all innocence, would tell Jennie about a real estate deal my mom was working on, and she would take the customer away. I don't know why, but Curly—like all his brothers—worshipped his mother.

JOAN: I have had various descriptions of Curly and what his personality was like. In the '40s he was described as being quiet—almost dull on the set. Can you recall what he was like when you knew him back in Pittsburgh?

BERNICE: When Uncle Babe stayed with us, he was never quiet, certainly not dull. Dinner time was great fun, as he was very gregarious. He was always "onstage" and loved to be funny.

JOAN: Was he ever vulgar?

BERNICE: Never around us—Dolly, Norman, and me. Of course, we were young children. I don't know how he was with the rest of the family.

JOAN: Do you think that Curly was as close to his parents as Shemp and Moe?

BERNICE: I'm sure he loved them, but he may not have been as attached to them, because he was the youngest, and at that time Jennie was getting to be a very busy woman.

JOAN: My father painted Jennie as the perfect mother, almost a saint, while others in the family have been less than kind. What were Jennie and Sol really like?

BERNICE: Grandma was the businesswoman. She was volatile while Grandpa was serene. He walked behind her, hardly able to keep up. Even though she had short legs and he long, she scurried along like a jackrabbit. She was like a mother dragging a child; she would pinch his upper arm and say, "Come, Sol." And you can bet he did! I recall that Grandpa, when he was alone, would always sit in the dark. [He was a frugal man and hated to waste electricity.] He did have a hearty laugh, and when something struck him funny, he shook like a bowl of Jell-O.

JOAN: How did Curly get along with his brothers?

BERNICE: All the boys watched over Curly. When he was very young, it was because he was the baby of the family; when he was older, it was to protect him from his surroundings. And your father did control him for a long time. Guess he always felt the "big brother" and was aware of Curly's sensitivity and lack of business acumen.

JOAN: Curly loved cars. Did he have a car in the old days?

BERNICE: He didn't have a car of his own in the early years but he did drive a big Hupmobile which was supplied by Jennie and Sol. Neither of them drove, so I imagine Curly chauffeured them around. He picked up many of the Bensonhurst girls while driving. He'd lean out the window and yell, "Hi, Toots!"

JOAN: Was Curly a well man in his early years?

BERNICE: Yes, Uncle Babe was never ill. He did have bad eating habits. Ate much too much and much too fast. I picked up this bad habit of his; he used to want to race with me during dinner to see who could finish first. Guess who won?

A month after interviewing Bernice, I located another cousin, my uncle Irving's youngest daughter, Margie Golden, whom I hadn't seen in over twenty-five years. It was only through some clever detective work and the help of the California Dental Association (Margie's husband, Harold, is a dentist) that I found out she was living within a mile of my house. I called my cousin Margie, who agreed to meet with me at her house, where she would answer my questions about our uncle Curly.

INTERVIEW

Courtesy of the subject

Margie Horwitz Golden

May 9, 1985

JOAN: Could you tell me what Jennie was like?

MARGIE: Grandma was the most wonderful—the best. The best grandmother anybody could have.

JOAN: What year was this?

MARGIE: I was about seven or eight. It must have been about 1929. It was the time that Jennie and Sol went to Europe for four months. And Curly went with them.

JOAN: I heard Jennie was going to Lithuania to see her family.

MARGIE: Yes, and she went to the baths in Baden-Baden.

JOAN: Through the years, I recall my dad saying that your father, Irving, was Jennie's favorite. Do you have any idea why?

MARGIE: He was a *Teller vom Himmel*.

JOAN: What does that mean?

MARGIE: A dish from heaven. That was what he was to her.

JOAN: Was this because he was the first son?

MARGIE: No, Jennie was very poor at the time—doing piecework, sewing little boys' pants in a basement. And Irving was born at a time when they were unable to give him things.

JOAN: I thought she might have cared for him more because he was frail.

MARGIE: He was delicate. I recall a story about Jennie and my father. One time Jennie was lying in bed with baby Irving. This was when she and Sol were living in an apartment. She fell asleep, and when she awoke, my father had crawled out of the bed and onto a ledge outside the window, which was several stories up. He was perched precariously, about to fall. Jennie crawled on all fours around the room toward the window, never saying a word, afraid she'd scare him. When she reached my father, she grabbed his foot and pulled him in.

JOAN: Goodness! How old was he then?

MARGIE: He was about two years old.

JOAN: I've heard several stories about our grandmother from members of the family. One cousin said she was a martinet.

MARGIE: She was quite a woman. Very tough. She used to send me to the store, and before I left, she would say, "Margie, you tell the man that Jennie Horwitz sent you. Remember, you don't have to pay anything. He'll trust you. Just tell him it's for Jennie Horwitz." And they trusted her.

JOAN: And Grandpa . . . was the quiet one. And definitely not a businessman.

MARGIE: He just collected the rents for her. Collected them and gave them to her. Everything was hers.

JOAN: Can you recall any humorous stories about Jennie and Sol?

MARGIE: Oh, yes. I remember going to Shemp's house with Grandma and Grandpa. And I'll never forget—Shemp and his wife, Babe, had bought live lobsters, and you know religious Jews are not supposed to eat shellfish. And so Shemp hid them by dumping them in the stall shower. We were all sitting in the kitchen, and Grandma and Grandpa could hear the click click of the lobsters' claws. And there was Shemp trying to cover things up by telling them all kinds of crazy stories, insisting it was mice.

JOAN: Did she ever see them?

MARGIE: [Laughing.] Oh, no. She would have died.

JOAN: My father said Jennie was a saint, and all the sons felt this way about her. But other members of the family thought of her as a shrewd, calculating businesswoman.

MARGIE: That was true, but she did everything for her children. She was a devoted mother.

JOAN: When Curly was born, Jennie was completely wrapped up in real estate. Did she have time for him?

MARGIE: He was on his own. He wouldn't listen to anybody.

JOAN: I heard Curly was married for the first time in New York in 1929. Can you give me any information about his wife?

MARGIE: I remember her. She was a very pretty girl, about two or three years younger than Curly.

JOAN: How could Jennie go to her son and make him divorce his wife?

MARGIE: Curly was about twenty-five. I don't think Curly's marriage broke up because of Jennie. I think something happened between him and his wife. It was probably his fault. I remember Curly used to take girls home in a taxi, and he'd tell the driver to stop off at his house first, as he needed to get money for the fare. He'd stop at a street around the corner from his house, and he'd go through the alley to his house, leaving the girl in the cab. He'd never come back, and she'd have to pay the fare. He was a devil—a real little devil.

JOAN: Did he work at all during this period?

MARGIE: Never—never. Never really worked a day in his life.

JOAN: I wonder why all Jennie's sons idolized her and listened to her. Did they fear her?

MARGIE: No—no. She never touched them. She did give them everything they needed. There wasn't much money to spread around, and she worked hard. She took old houses and barns and fixed them up, and my father [Irving] would sell them. This was before he went into the insurance business.

JOAN: Do you recall how Curly got that deep scar on his cheek?

MARGIE: Yes. He was in an automobile accident. He was in the Hupmobile, and a streetcar ran right into it. Curly was about twenty-one and he almost died.

JOAN: I got the feeling that Curly could have been a careless kid or had poor judgment.

MARGIE: I don't know about that, but he did have idiosyncrasies. I know he never stayed in the house alone unless the lights were on. Every light had to be on when he was home.

JOAN: Was he a well man at that time?

MARGIE: His health seemed OK, but I got the feeling that he was a very unhappy man.

JOAN: Can you tell me more about Sol?

MARGIE: I remember a cute story that happened one Passover. Grandpa was sitting on the cushions at the seder and reading the service—and it usually took several hours—and

To My Brother
"Irving"
From Your
Loveing Brother
"Babe"
Nov. 16, 1933.

Portrait of a very handsome Curly. Evident on his cheek is the scar from his car accident (1933).

all the boys were sitting around the table. They were starving. It was after 9:00 PM, and they still hadn't served dinner. When Grandpa got up to wash his hands, Shemp jumped up and flipped the pages in Sol's book. When he got back to the table, he went right on reading from the new spot that Shemp had turned to, never realizing what had happened. Shemp did this several times during the service, and, boy, did it go fast!

JOAN: Did Jennie ever put hundred-dollar bills under the kids' plates?

MARGIE: I don't know, but she did give me fifty cents once, and I thought I was rich. It only took a dime in those days to go to the movies. I remember one time—we had a Victrola—and Curly would put my feet on top of his shoes and dance around the room with me.

JOAN: I heard he was a wonderful dancer.

MARGIE: He was, he was—very light on his feet. And he had a nice voice, too.

JOAN: I have the feeling that Jennie took Curly to Europe to keep an eye on him, and not only to keep him out of show business, but to keep him away from his first wife.

MARGIE: Curly really liked that first wife. He was nuts about her. I think it really crushed him.

JOAN: I heard two stories about the first wife. One was that she was Gentile, the other that she was Jewish.

MARGIE: I'm sure she was Jewish.

JOAN: A lot of people said Curly was very vulgar.

MARGIE: He was vulgar, all right. He used a lot of four-letter words. My mother used to clap her hands over my ears when he would start to talk. But he was wonderful to me. One time he gave me five dollars, and it took me a whole year to spend it.

JOAN: Do you recall any of Curly's likes or dislikes?

MARGIE: He liked to drink. He went out a lot. He'd come home and shower and get dressed, put on cologne and perfume. [*Margie stops and lets out a cry.*] *Pauline*—that's her name, Pauline.

JOAN: The first wife? You're sure?

MARGIE: Yes. Pauline.

JOAN: Do you think you could dredge up the last name?

MARGIE: No.

JOAN: Tell me more about Curly's first wife.

MARGIE: I only saw her once, for a short time when Grandma lived on Eighty-Second Street. They [Jennie and Sol] had a beautiful house with a piano and everything. The first wife was there with Curly. He had married her and brought her over to introduce her to Grandma.

JOAN: Was this a surprise to Jennie?

MARGIE: Oh, of course it was. Now, I wonder—if she was Jewish.

JOAN: You seemed to like Jennie.

MARGIE: Yes. She was a wonderful woman; she was a crackerjack!

At the end of our conversation, Margie reminded me about her sister Ruth, who lived in Florida. Since she was several years older than Margie, I thought there might be a good chance she could recall something about Curly's first wife; I was hoping to find out her last name. It took about six phone calls to reach Ruth. First I dialed three wrong numbers, after which I called her daughter Bonnie, a young woman in her thirties, who lives not far from me in Santa Monica. She sounded delightful and gave me her mother's new phone number, and we made plans to get together.

Finally, at about six in the evening on Mother's Day, I reached Ruth. I found out right off that her recall was not like her sister's, but she did have several pertinent things to say.

INTERVIEW

Courtesy of the subject

Ruth Horwitz Leibowitz Kramer

May 12, 1985

JOAN: Margie told me a great deal about our grandmother, Jennie, whom I never really knew. What did you think of her?

RUTH: She was the sweetest—the sweetest. But she was a very tough businesswoman. Nobody got away with anything where Jennie was concerned. If she went to the butcher and he wanted Jennie for a customer, he had to give to her pet charities. With Jennie, you had to do her a favor in order to get a favor.

JOAN: I heard her children were very devoted to her.

RUTH: My father, Irving, was her favorite. Although sometimes she'd say one of the other sons was her favorite.

JOAN: What else do you remember about the Horwitz brothers?

RUTH: I recall several of the boys used to help her with the housework—like little girls. Curly never helped.

JOAN: Did he ever work?

RUTH: [Hearty laughter.] I don't think so. I remember his eyes. They used to fascinate me. He had the bluest eyes. He was quite good-looking before he shaved his head.

JOAN: Do you recall his ever playing the piano?

RUTH: I only remember the spoons.

JOAN: You are about the fifth interviewee who has mentioned that. I don't know if you know it, but he graduated from playing the spoons to ripping tablecloths.

RUTH: Really? He was very good-natured and very free with his money. When he came to visit, he brought my kids roller-skates. He used to hang around the poolrooms—not always with the nicest young men. And he gave Grandma lots and lots of trouble as a youngster.

JOAN: Trouble? What kind of trouble?

RUTH: He used to tell me that he didn't graduate from school, Grandma did. That Grandma went to school more than he did.

Solomon Horwitz with his granddaughter Ruth (1922).

JOAN: Poor Jennie. I heard that Shemp played a great deal of hooky, too. Oh, yes, someone also described Curly as a loner. When I say loner, I mean not having any close friends but hating to be alone. Is that true?

RUTH: Yes. He had an obsession about being alone. A phobia—almost a fear.

When Curly returned to New York from his Pittsburgh visit with Bernice and her family, he was surprised to find Jennie nervous and uptight. The tentacles of the Great Depression were closing in. Unemployment was rampant, land was just not selling, and burdened with dozens of mortgages on her properties, she was about to have the bottom fall out of her real estate enterprises.

Although Jennie's world was about to tumble, the Great Depression of the '30 would be a golden era for Curly. He would continue with Orville Knapp for several more years of waving his baton and losing his pants—and then lady luck would step in and change his life forever.

4

THE '30s

Curly Meets Life Head-On with a Shaven Head • And Then There Were Three • Exit Ted Healy, Enter Columbia • Marriage #2 and Daughter #1 • Europe and George White's Scandals

Where his life was concerned, Curly was still not in the driver's seat. Jennie continued to rule him with her iron hand, and much of Curly's days were spent behind the wheel of the Horwitz Hupmobile, chauffeuring his busy mother all over town.

One of the highlights of 1930 was a visit by Sol's sister Esther and her daughter, Emily, who had come in from St. Paul. Curly was elected to squire them around. This was the same Esther who was the household servant Jennie had imported from Lithuania in the Bath Beach days.

Her daughter, Emily, was a beautiful young girl, and Curly, for the first time, looked forward with pleasure to driving someone about the city. His pleasure was doubled when his mother explained that she had tickets for the theater and they would all be going to Manhattan to see Moe and Shemp in their latest vaudeville extravaganza.

Jennie was in a generous mood and, possibly feeling remorse over her past treatment of Esther, seemed honestly concerned with showing her sister-in-law and her niece a good time. She had made plans to take them to dinner in a fine New York restaurant, and Moe had taken care of getting them all house seats.

Jennie's royal treatment of her relatives began with an incredible drive down the Great White Way, along its fairyland of sparkling lights. Emily and Esther were impressed, and the sights and sounds and glitter of Broadway were things that Curly never tired of. Being a part of it was his constant dream, and his imagination always went wild when he visited the area. Then, as he rounded a corner, there was the epitome of theaters—the Palace—and up on the brightly lit marquee, headlining the bill, for all to see, was his brothers' star billing: TED HEALY AND HIS RACKETEERS.

Inside the legendary theater, Curly watched bug-eyed from fifth row center as Ted Healy, who always came onstage with a battered hat—his trademark—banged and pounded his Racketeers. Healy's stooges at the time consisted of four members: There were Curly's brothers, Moe and Shemp Howard, and their partner, Larry Fine, who had been with the team since 1928, when he was discovered in a Chicago club doing a Russian dance in high hat and tails while playing the violin. The fourth team member, newcomer xylophonist Fred Sanborn, was with the team for a very short time. The Racketeers were a motley crew, but they performed their zany Stooge antics with precision timing, taking the brunt of Healy's roughhouse humor and physical abuse. It was a wild, slapstick performance marked with crudity, and the audience ate it up.

My cousin Emily Trager, who was with the family at the Palace that night, told me, "The audience laughed so hard that in order to keep their patrons from choking, the theater owners had ushers running up and down the aisles serving water. Curly laughed so hard that he had two full glasses, but uptight Jennie didn't require a single drop. She sat stone-faced through the entire performance and never even cracked a smile."

Curly that evening was like a man gone mad, dying to get up on that stage, to be the center of attention. His mind raced with both jealousy and frustration at being on the edge of the spotlight and not illuminated by it as Moe and Shemp were. At home, later that night, he pleaded with Jennie to allow him to go into show business full-time.

Jennie was an expert at camouflaging her iron hand with a velvet glove. "Who would take me to the Home for the Aged? Who would take poor Sol to shul?" she pleaded. Jennie claimed that she desperately needed him, and Curly, no match for this clever little woman of steel, gave in. But deep down he had made up his mind. There would be no college or trade school for him. He would bide his time, watch his brothers' act, and study their style until he had it down pat. When the time was right, he'd be waiting in the wings, Jennie or no Jennie.

Ted Healy and His Racketeers, circa 1930. Larry, Moe, Shemp, and Fred Sanborn in a scene from Fox's film *Soup to Nuts* (1930).

Night after night he would drive to the theater and sit there absorbing every nuance until, suddenly, his watching and studying of Healy and his Stooges came to an abrupt halt. A talent scout from Fox Studios saw the act at the Palace and hired Ted and his Racketeers for Fox's new feature film *Soup to Nuts*, written by the famous cartoonist Rube Goldberg. Two of the Horwitz boys had finally made it to the "big time" and would soon be Hollywood bound.

The following week, Curly drove Moe, Shemp, and their families to Grand Central Station, where he witnessed their elation as they waved from the rear platform and the train chugged out of the station, taking them all to Hollywood. When he returned home to Brooklyn, he was in a state of depression, wondering when it would be his turn and what it must feel like to be a movie star.

Curly, his show business dreams and ambitions in a holding pattern, waited patiently for his brothers to return. It was late in 1930 when he received his first letter from Moe, explaining the details of what had taken place in Hollywood during the past several months. Moe's letter related how the Stooges' stint in *Soup to Nuts* was well received by both the press and the studio heads and Healy had come off second-best. Only Moe, Larry, and Shemp were offered a contract with Fox. Then, several days later, the contract was canceled. It didn't take Moe long

Ted Healy and His Three Southern
Gentlemen, circa 1930.

Papa Moe, Momma Helen, and the author, on tour in
Seattle, Washington (1930).

to realize that they had been betrayed by Healy, who had gone to his old pal Winnie Sheehan, the production head of Fox, and coerced him into canceling the Stooges' contract. It was both fear of losing his act and jealousy that had driven Healy to cut the Stooges' throats. Because of this incident, Larry, Moe, and Shemp refused to continue their association with Ted.

As he read the rest of Moe's letter, Curly found it hard to believe that Larry and his brothers would be working without Healy and that they would open at the Paramount Theater in Los Angeles. In closing, Moe wrote that they would take their new act across the country, using most of the material from their old routines with Healy, but were changing their names to the Three Lost Souls.

The weeks dragged into months, and Curly was learning patience with a capital *P*. He would need it. Moe and Shemp would not return to New York City until late in 1931. Their personal appearances would keep them busy for months, and weeks would be spent in a California courtroom, when Ted Healy sued them for using his material in their new act.

More letters to Curly followed, and in September Moe wrote to him that they had won their lawsuit with Healy. In closing, Moe penned, "Healy is desperate to get us back. His replacement stooges were a terrible disappointment to him. He has promised to stop drinking

Shemp portrait (1930).

and I hope we're not making a mistake but we've decided to go back to him. We'll be arriving in New York next month for rehearsals for the new Shubert musical, *The Passing Show of 1932.* Your loving brother, Moe."

Weeks later, Curly received a call from Shemp, who cried on his shoulder, telling him that he was fed up with Healy. They had rehearsed *The Passing Show* for four weeks, and then Ted and Shubert had an argument over salary. When Ted found a loophole in his contract, he decided to leave Shubert to take a more lucrative offer from the Balaban & Katz circuit.

Shemp was sick of Healy's deviousness, his alcoholism, and his cruel practical jokes. He confided in Curly, "To tell you the truth, I'm afraid of him, and I've decided to let Healy leave with Moe and Larry. I'm going to stay in the Shubert show."

Then Shemp dropped a bomb that exploded happily in Curly's ears: "It's possible Moe and Larry will be looking for a replacement for me. They need a third stooge!"

Ted, Shemp, Moe, and Larry at the stage door, circa 1931.

Curly's older
brother Irving
and his wife,
Nettie, visiting
the Stooges in
Atlantic City
(1931).

A third stooge! Curly went mad with excitement. Was this his long-awaited chance to become a star? At that glorious moment, if he knew how to do it, he might have woo-wooed and n'yuk-n'yuked at the top of his lungs. Instead, he started to laugh hysterically.

When Curly regained his composure, he called Moe, who corroborated Shemp's story, adding that Healy was furious—out to kill—and had accused Shemp of trying to destroy the act. Moe then said, "Healy asked me who was going to replace Shemp. I told him that I'd call my brother Jerome. Babe, you have an appointment with Ted Healy tomorrow at two o'clock."

Curly was beside himself with joy. He wanted to shout the news throughout the house, but he feared that his mother would never understand. Instead, he went straight to the Triangle Ballroom, downed a dozen beers, and danced until dawn.

The next morning, when he awoke, he had a bad case of the jitters. Would Healy accept him? He had so little stage experience. The only professional work he'd done was dropping his pants for Orville Knapp. But he had studied Shemp and Moe's act for the last few months and had followed them around for years, and he knew their routines backward and forward. The odds, he thought, were in his favor, and he was determined to prove to Healy that he would make the world's greatest stooge.

The meeting with Healy started out disastrously. Moe was rooting for him so hard that his nervousness was engraved on his face and infected Curly. When Healy asked Curly what he could do, Curly croaked out, "I don't know." And then Healy retorted with, "Well, I know what you can do. You can shave your head."

Curly chuckled at what he was certain was one of Healy's sick jokes. Then Healy turned to Moe and Larry Fine and said, "Look, boys, he looks too normal with his wavy hair and waxed mustache. Moe, you have this spittoon haircut, and Larry, you look like a scared porcupine." Then he turned to Curly and said, "You just don't fit in."

The meeting ended, and Curly went home feeling sad and beaten. Alone in his room, he started to think maybe Healy wasn't joking. Maybe he should shave his head. The thought repelled him. The only things that made his life worth living were music and girls. How could he go to the Triangle with a shaved head? And what would his friends think? God! What would Jennie think? But he wanted this job like life itself. This was the point of no return. The hell with everyone.

Curly woke up the next morning feeling hungover, although he hadn't had a thing to drink. But like a drunk in a stupor, he dragged himself to the barber, cap in hand, knowing that he wouldn't be able to face the world again without something covering his head.

In the barbershop, Curly blurted out instructions for his haircut, shouting, "Shave my head—shave it right down to the bone." Having meticulously trimmed Curly's hair for several years, his barber wouldn't have been any more surprised if he had said, "Take your razor and slit my throat."

It took some convincing to assure the barber that this was no joke, and finally the clippers whirred ominously as they mowed their way through his wavy locks. For minutes that seemed like hours, Curly felt as though he were undergoing major surgery. Then he took one glance at the bald-headed stranger in the mirror staring back at him, and one glance was enough. He quickly paid his tab, grabbed his cap, jammed it down over his head, and dashed out.

Interior of the Hotel Paramount Grill (1932).

Promotion poster for Curly's appearance at the Hotel Paramount Grill (1932).

The next meeting with Healy was markedly different. Curly had everything planned, right down to his grand entrance. An impressed Healy watched as Curly ambled in, skipping along, looking like a fat fairy. When he pulled off his cap, it took only seconds for a grinning Healy to say, "You're in, Jerry." With tears of joy rolling down his cheeks, my uncle blurted out, "If you want me, call me Curly."

He'd done it. He was finally in, and there was no turning back. From here on, Jerome/Jerry/Babe Horwitz would forever be just plain Curly to millions of theatergoers and an army of loyal fans, most of whom were yet unborn.

That same week in 1933, the traditional Friday-night dinner at Jennie's was a traumatic event for our new Stooge. Curly sat down at his mother's table with his little cap pulled down hard over his head, wishing that Shemp and Moe were there, because they knew how to handle Jennie better than he did. Sol was already seated, his yarmulke on his head, meticulously slicing the challah on the plate in front of him. Jennie entered, scowling as she stared at Curly's cap pulled down rakishly over his ears. He knew that he would have to remove it and replace it with his traditional little blue velvet yarmulke, which would expose his Spartan skull. What would his mother's reaction be when she glimpsed his shiny bald head? The thought panicked him. This was showdown time—time to be his own man. He whipped off his cap and Jennie screamed. She literally jumped out of her chair and shrieked in horror at the top of her lungs. Curly felt as though he were drowning. He was speechless—in a state of shock equal to, if not surpassing, Jennie's. Finally, when the words did come, they were totally scrambled. "Mom," he stuttered, "I'm a stooge—I'm actually a stooge. Don't worry. It'll grow, and you'll grow to love it."

With that, Jennie started to cry. "I knew it! I knew that this show business thing was a curse."

Curly stood up and moved closer to her, searching for a way to soothe her anguish. He felt terrible. Jennie had done so much for him through the years, given him everything he ever wanted. He couldn't hold her close, because there were never hugs and kisses in the Horwitz family, but he always knew the love was there. His father sat like a stone, staring at them, never saying a word but with a hint of a grin on his face. Then Sol, who rarely ever spoke, said softly, "I envy you, my son. You have something now that will give your life meaning." Both Jennie and Curly stared at him, and words failed them. That was the most that either had ever heard Sol say at any one time. It broke the tension of the moment and made Curly feel better. He grabbed his blue velvet yarmulke and, with a flourish, slapped it over his shaved skull, and the three finished their dinners in silence.

The biggest hurdle in Curly's young life was over. He had finally severed the cord. Curly, who had changed his last name to Howard, was in show business at last, and his domineering mother would have to learn to accept it.

And then came the usual doubts, heartaches, and problems that plague most neophytes in any profession. During the first few weeks of his new career. Curly noticed that Healy was reticent about letting him use any of Shemp's material, which he had studied for months and knew by heart. Healy was concerned about Curly's inexperience, and in the beginning all he allowed him to do was run across the stage in a tight-fitting bathing suit, carrying a little pail of water. It was a hysterically funny sight—this fat, bald Humpty Dumpty of a man skittering about half-naked with his little dripping pail—but Curly was still frustrated. He knew he could do more and could get even bigger laughs from the audience.

Each night the laughter increased as Curly, gaining assurance with every laugh, milked his routine for all it was worth. With each succeeding performance, he sneaked in a line or two of Shemp's routines and, as he anticipated, the audience howled even louder. Healy was an astute showman and, knowing a good thing when he saw it, eventually gave his new Stooge free rein. Curly, through his own ingenuity, had worked his way into the act and had become a full-fledged comedian.

By the time Healy and His Stooges played the Club New Yorker in Hollywood's Christie Hotel, Curly had taken over Shemp's role completely, added his own incredible touches, and become the best stooge Healy ever had. It was there, in this basement nightclub, that an MGM

Ted Healy and His
Stooges at the Club New
Yorker in Hollywood's
Christie Hotel. It was
during this engagement
that an earthquake
wrecked the nightclub
(1933).

scout watched the performance of Ted Healy and His Stooges for the first time and was impressed. Then, as their act ended and the audience applauded, the entire room shook. But it wasn't only from the applause; chandeliers swayed and the room rocked as plaster and dust plummeted from the ceiling. This was the 1933 Long Beach earthquake, which sent its shock waves throughout Los Angeles. It was an unforgettable night for everyone present at the Club New Yorker, and especially for the Stooges, who were signed up on the spot to a one-year contract by the MGM scout.

For Curly, 1933 was a dream come true. For the time being he would have no regrets about that traumatic day at his barber when he shaved his head. He was among the stars: Garbo, Gable, Crawford—the cream of the movie industry. Curly was a star now, too, and with it came adulation, girls, applause. This was Hollywood in its heyday, and Curly was finally a part of it.

The Stooges' first feature appearance was in MGM's *Turn Back the Clock*, with Lee Tracy and Mae Clarke. This was followed by *Meet the Baron*, with Jimmy Durante, and then *Dancing Lady*, *Fugitive Lovers*, and *Hollywood Party*. Healy and His Stooges were on a roll, also starring in five MGM musical-comedy shorts, the first of which, *Nertsery Rhymes*, was released in two-strip experimental color.

Curly, Moe, and Larry
harmonize with Ted Healy
in *Dancing Lady* (1933).

Curly was on cloud nine when he read his reviews, and always the thoughtful son, he wanted to share his joy with his mother. He sent her a clipping of a wonderful review of *Nertsery Rhymes* and informed her of the date it would be playing in the Horwitzes' neighborhood theater in Brooklyn.

On a summer's day in 1933, Jennie, who had often seen Moe and Shemp slapping and poking each other on the live vaudeville stage and always shivered at the sight, had never seen any of her sons on the silver screen, so she marked her calendar and decided to attend the theater at an afternoon matinee.

This staid, stern Victorian woman sat in the front row and struggled to ignore the screaming kids who raced up and down the aisles tossing popcorn or anything they could get their hands on at each other and at the screen as they waited for the show to start.

Suddenly, the house lights dimmed and the screaming and whistling of the kids accelerated as the MGM lion roared and the title flashed on: TED HEALY AND HIS STOOGES IN *NERTSERY RHYMES*.

Onto the screen, larger than life, came Ted, Larry, and then finally Moe and Curly. Jennie stared ahead, her face frozen into impassivity as hammers and mallets were swung at her boys, with most of the blows landing on the head of her baby, Curly. The exaggerated sound effects and the ear-shattering *clang*s and *boing*s were frighteningly realistic to her.

Ted Healy and His Stooges, with Bonnie Bonnell, in MGM's *Nertsery Rhymes* (1933).

As this incredible on-screen mayhem increased in intensity, Jennie became more and more agitated and, unable to hold back her emotions, began to mutter under her breath in a mixture of English and Yiddish: "Vey—you crazy idiots! To Hollywood you had to go to kill each other." Then she totally lost control and, recalling her sons' vaudeville act—which she hated—screamed, "Not enough you should poke fingers in the eyes, now you gotta use clubs and hammers." Ignoring the kids in the nearby seats who stared at her, she continued shouting at the screen: "Moe, you no-goodnik! That's your baby brother Babe you're smashing! For this I slaved all my life—so my sons should be movie stars. Feh!"

Unable to contain herself and totally frustrated, she bolted from her seat and charged up to the stage, waving her umbrella menacingly at the screen, and in a hysterical voice screamed, "A pox on you, Ted Healy!"

Moments later, poor, old-world Jennie was still muttering under her breath in her broken English as the confused usher took her gently by the arm and escorted her out of the theater.

ce Runs 'Bill of Divorcement'
·liss Comedy Heads Capitol

Ted Healy's Troupe Seen At Rochester

LOEW'S Rochester Theater offers another week of big name vaudeville. Ted Healy, the nonchalant comedian of stage and screen, heads the current stage show. Metro-Goldwyn-Mayer's picture of the African jungle, "Kongo," is the screen attraction.

Healy is remembered for the dilapidated hat he always wears, and about which there is much speculation as to whether it is always the same one. Many as a matter of fact, hang on the wall of his dressing room. Healy is one of the most informal of comedians. His naturalness makes for his success.

Aileen Stanley croons a group of songs, each song a sketch, for Miss Stanley is an actress, too, it is said. Gordon, Reed and King billed as "Three Gentlemen from Manhattan;" the Five Elgins in "Making Themselves at Home," and Ted Healy with His Gang of Racketeers will complete the stage bill.

In "Kongo" Walter Huston plays the role of a half-crazed white man who has become ruler over a tribe of savage natives in the Kongo. He keeps them under his control by the use of "black magic." They fear his every move. He has drawn several white members into his kingdom. Over these he rules with fear of his whip.

He sends out of the jungle to steal a girl whom he wishes to make suffer, thinking she is the daughter of a man who wronged him. He keeps her in the jungle

Ted Healy and His Gang, stage comedians, at Loew's Rochester.

News clipping of Ted Healy and His Gang (1932). Curly, with shaven head, still sports his mustache.

Despite Curly's love for this magical world of showbiz, his shaved head would always diminish his confidence in his appearance. He constantly wore a hat and, to give himself a bit of needed courage, would always belt down a few quick ones before approaching the fairer sex. During vaudeville tours, after he would finish taking his nocturnal beatings onstage, the local nightspots were his home. He still loved music, and a drumbeat or a bouncy number would always start his feet to tapping. Many evenings at a nightclub, when he was feeling no pain, he would take the edge of a tablecloth between his thumbs and forefingers and rip the fabric to the tempo of the music. After the tablecloth was in shreds, he'd take two spoons and click the backs together until the silver plating was covered with dents. Curly was able to make those two spoons sound like a pair of castanets, and there were often times when he would actually jump up on the bandstand, grab the bass fiddle out of the hands of a shocked musician, and plunk away as well as any professional. Throughout his life, Curly was always a night owl, and much of his salary would be squandered in order to pay for shredded tablecloths, pockmarked silverware, and broken bass strings.

Paying off nightclub owners and struggling to overcome the trauma of his shaven head were minor problems in Curly's life in these heady days. Greater concern centered on his parents. The country was in the grips of a major depression, and Jennie—mortgaged to the hilt with her many real estate holdings—was on the verge of bankruptcy.

POSED BY TED HEALY AND HIS STOOGES IN "BACK-STAGE," A METRO-GOLDWYN-MAYER COMEDY.

"As actors you guys are lousy. But I know how we can make some real money. I'll make you all prize fighters and invest five hundred in your first fights."

"In training?"

"No, in betting on your opponents."

Curly in Hollywood—with Moe, Larry, and Ted Healy onstage at MGM (1933).

(*Below, left*) News clipping of MGM's *Dancing Lady* with Crawford and Gable . . . and Healy and His Stooges (1933)

(*Below, right*) *Hollywood Party* (MGM) news clipping. Ted Healy and His Stooges get billing above Mickey Mouse (1933).

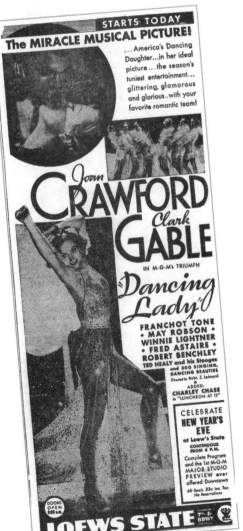

Curly with Edna May Oliver in a publicity still from MGM's *Meet the Baron* (1933).

Curly in a rare solo performance in MGM's *Roast-Beef and Movies*, with George Givot and Joe Callahan (1933).

Moe and Curly rough up Momma Jennie and Poppa Sol as they arrive in California for the first time (1933).

Curly, center, with his favorite people—Mabel, Larry, Moe, and Helen (1933).

Helen, Moe, and Curly clowning at a friend's beach house (1933).

Publicity shot of the Stooges, circa 1933.

LAST MINUTE PHOTOS
(CHANGED DAILY)

THREE STOOGES!

Hollywood, Calif.—Here's how Hollywood stooges go in for summer attire. Jerry Howard, Moe Howard and Larry Fine, who make a living as stooges, are shown walking down the boulevard attired in white shorts and sporting a "man-sized" umbrella.

INTERNATIONAL NEWS PHOTO.

PICTURE FROM THE
Herald Chicago and Examiner
CHICAGO'S MOST INTERESTING NEWSPAPER

MGM back lot (1934).

A dream come true: Curly's new home, Hollywood, 1934. *Bison Archives*

Curly and the boys attempt to hammer some sense into Bonnie and Ted.

Added to his concern for Jennie was his concern for his favorite brother, Moe, who was showing signs of discontent, brought about by Healy's unfair treatment of his Stooges. Healy had reneged on his promises to reform and was still drinking heavily and playing outrageous practical jokes. That was bad enough, but Healy, although he was earning several thousand dollars a week as payment for the act, including his three Stooges, was still paying them their original salary of only one hundred dollars a week.

Despite the fact that Healy was a talented performer on his own, every review singled out the Stooges as having made the act something special. When Moe digested the full meaning of the positive press that he and his partners were getting in both California and New York, he finally got up enough courage to sever the cord with Ted. He confronted Healy at MGM and amicably put an end to their long relationship. It was 1934, and the Stooges, for better or worse, were ready to strike out on their own.

The details of Moe, Curly, and Larry's parting of the ways with Ted Healy and then signing their contract with Columbia in 1934 had all the makings of a movie script. After the final meeting with Healy, Moe walked out of one MGM gate and signed a contract for the Three Stooges with Columbia Pictures, totally unaware that Larry had left from another MGM gate and signed another contract for the Three Stooges with Universal Studios. The two contracts went to the lawyers of Columbia and Universal and finally to a judge. In the end, the evidence indicated that Moe's Columbia contract was signed several hours before Larry put his signature to Universal's. Columbia got the Stooges, and Larry would never again, for the next half century, ever conduct any of the Three Stooges' business.

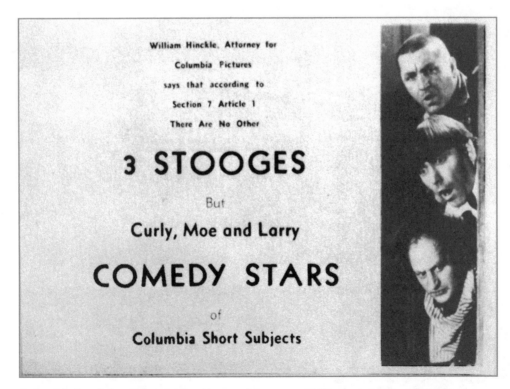

Columbia legal department advertisement to warn off Stooge infringers (1936).

Moe had taken over completely as manager of the Stooges' act, and Curly, forever busy buying shiny new cars and driving down Hollywood Boulevard yelling "Hiya, toots!" at every pair of pretty legs, was satisfied to let him handle all business matters for the act as well as personal matters for himself.

Curly had become a major star in the Short Subjects Department at Columbia Studio and made his first film, *Woman Haters*, a musical comedy all in rhyme. Although this was Curly's first Columbia short, it was not a Three Stooges comedy as we know them today. The boys were not yet known as the Three Stooges or working together as Larry, Moe, and Curly. In this film, Curly and Moe appear as supporting players, with Larry in the role of the leading man. It wasn't until June 1, 1934, that the three officially took on the name "the Three Stooges."

One of Curly's favorite hangouts, the Cafe Trocadero on the fabulous Sunset Strip (1934). *Bison Archives*

The Columbia Ranch western street in 1934, where most of the Curly shorts were filmed. *Bison Archives*

Moe clowns around trimming Curly's hairless head in a dressing room at Columbia Studio. Note Curly's faithful hat on his shelf (1934).

To our darling Cousins "Emily & Al." from Moe & Babe.

A publicity still sent by Curly and Moe to their cousin Emily and her husband, Al (1934).

Clarence Bull / MGM

After completing *Woman Haters*, Curly and his partners waited nervously for word from Columbia's executive office as to whether they would be hired to make another film. Then Moe, impatient to go back to work, came up with a wacky story idea for a short titled *Punch Drunks* and submitted it to the Columbia executives. The studio was so impressed with his original story that they signed the trio to a seven-year contract with yearly options. The Stooges would make eight shorts each year for Columbia with a twelve-week layoff period to perform in any entertainment category except making films for other studios. Curly was thrilled when his $333-a-week paycheck, which was a great deal of money in the '30s, was suddenly raised to a whopping four-figure salary. He felt like a millionaire and spent like crazy, and Moe had his hands full struggling to hold him down and make him save for the proverbial rainy day. But it was a losing battle. Curly was in the big time and living big. Wine, women, song, cars, dogs, and houses were there for the taking, and Curly managed to spend his entire weekly check before it was even handed to him.

In the ensuing years, Curly would perform in ninety-seven Three Stooges comedies for Columbia. Most of the films were quite violent, and the bruises that Curly endured were many. It's amazing he survived the battering, in which his bald dome took the brunt of the punishment—be it squashed in a printing press, slammed into a doorjamb, or sliced by a scimitar. If the *Guinness Book of Records* had a category for bops, bangs, and bruises received in the line of work, Curly would certainly hold the world record.

In one short, he was supposed to fall down an elevator shaft. A hole deep enough for Curly to be concealed from the camera after he landed was constructed in the stage floor. The special-effects man covered the bottom with a protective mattress to soften the impact but neglected to cover the sides of the opening, which were constructed with exposed two-by-fours. When Curly was pushed into the elevator shaft, his head hit the wooden framework, cutting his scalp wide open. The studio doctor rushed to the set, where he washed Curly's wound and sealed it with collodion. It was an example of the old saying "The show must go on." Minutes later, the head of the makeup department was rushed to the set to cover the wound with makeup, and a wobbly-legged Curly continued with his scene as if nothing had happened. Life was rough for the superstooge in front of the cameras and equally rough during the eleven years he performed onstage.

In addition to the multitude of bangs and bops that Curly received on hundreds of theater stages across America, much of his trouble during vaudeville tours came from drunks and children. They had often seen Curly take horrendous screen punishment and, like Jennie, believed what they saw and were convinced that Curly was made of steel.

Drunks would often stagger up to him and shout "Hiya, Curly!" and then smack him hard on his famous indestructible bald head. Children, at times, could be even more of a problem, because an impressionable child who had seen him clobbered on the screen wasn't mature enough to realize that lethal props such as hammers, crowbars, and sledges were made of foam rubber. Once in Atlantic City, when Curly was on the Boardwalk, lost in his thoughts, staring at the ocean, an eight-year-old boy carrying a small cane recognized him. "Look, Ma," he cried.

Larry and Moe showing off their rings to a ringless Curly. Publicity shot (1935).

"'There's one of the Three Stooges." Running up behind Curly, he took a tremendous swing and conked him over the head with his cane. Whirling around, Curly faced the young fan with glazed eyes, wobbly legs, and clenched fists. Then he noticed the boy's heavyset mother, beaming, grinning at her son as if proud that her kid had bopped the indestructible Stooge. Curly was momentarily taken aback. Regaining his composure, he smiled, took a cute Curly-style bow, and then grasped the railing next to him for support as his legs buckled.

The Stooges are billed above the marquee at the RKO Palace Theater—even above Bette Davis (1936). Notice the old spelling of *Curly* (Curley).

Larry and Curly charm Mildred Harris with their music in *Movie Maniacs* (1936).

This Boardwalk incident took place in 1935, the same year that Curly's parents went bust. The real estate bubble had burst, and Curly wrote Jennie and Sol and begged them to move to California. To Jennie, only Brooklyn was America and God's country, and despite her monumental financial setback, she refused to leave. It took a great deal of Curly and Moe's convincing to get her to relent and emigrate from her cherished Bensonhurst. In 1937 she finally agreed to make the move west, and her two famous sons pooled their resources and set their parents up in a lovely home on the edge of Beverly Hills.

In her sixties and suffering from high blood pressure, Jennie was not able to fully enjoy her new California home. I vividly recall my visits to my grandparents' as a ten-year-old. The house was always dark, with all the windows closed and the shades drawn. The air was extremely close inside and often smelled of sickness.

Despite the fact that Jennie was seriously ill, my grandfather, Sol, was still able to get around and would take a bus to downtown Los Angeles and visit with some of his Brooklyn cronies who had also moved to California. On one of his visits he was introduced to a very pretty dark-haired young Jewish girl, Elaine Ackerman. Impressed with her, he decided to play cupid for his son Curly. However, Sol's arrow missed its mark. Elaine was not interested in a blind date and refused to meet his son. But fate moves in strange ways. By an unusual coincidence (described later in an interview with Elaine), she wound up on a date with Curly shortly thereafter, and it was love at first sight—sort of.

Elaine soon became Curly's second wife in a simple ceremony in my grandparents' temple in Hollywood. Shemp, Moe, Larry, and their families were there, and Jennie left her sickbed to join the festivities.

Stooge 'Curly' Howard, L.A. Girl Reveal Troth

JERRY 'CURLY' HOWARD AND HIS FIANCEE,
ELAINE ACKERMAN
One of 'Three Stooges' to Wed Los Angeles Girl in June

The only bachelor among Hollywood's famous Three Stooges is about to give up single blessedness for marital happiness. He is Jerry "Curly" Howard, the roly-poly one.

A romance of less than two months culminated today with the announcement of the engagement of Elaine Ackerman of Los Angeles to "Curly." They will be married in June.

Elaine, who is a non-professional, saw the Stooges in a Columbia comedy about seven weeks ago. She laughed so much she went back to see it again. A week later she was introduced to them at the Hollywood home of a friend. Jerry made her laugh again. In fact, she laughed herself right into accepting a proposal of marriage.

Miss Ackerman is the daughter of Mr. and Mrs. Isadore Ackerman, 339 North Detroit street. Her father is a Los Angeles jeweler. Jerry is the son of Mr. and Mrs. Sol Howard. With Moe Howard and Larry Fine he has helped to put the word "Stooge" into the English language.

The wedding of Miss Ackerman and Howard will take place just before the team leaves on its annual personal appearance tour of the country. The trip will be a combined business tour and honeymoon. Upon their return the couple will live in a home to be built for them in the Toluca Lake district.

Curly and Elaine showing off her engagement ring to a smiling Jennie and blasé Sol (1937).

Curly and Elaine at their engagement party (1937).

Curly beams as Momma Jennie and bride Elaine greet each other at his wedding reception (1937).

Curly waits impatiently for the tardy rabbi to show up and tie the knot (1937).

The author on the receiving line at her uncle Curly's and aunt Elaine's wedding (1937).

Curly, Shemp, and Moe rough up their father on Curly's wedding day (1937).

Shemp's wife, Babe, on the receiving line at Curly's wedding to Elaine (1937).

Elaine poses with her new in-laws, Sol and Jennie, on her wedding day (1937).

Elaine poses in front of her Reno, Nevada, cabin on her honeymoon in 1937.

The Curly residence, one of many, on Highland Avenue in Hollywood, where he lived with Elaine.

The Stooges clown around with Curly's new bride, Elaine, in Curly's new home.

As for Elaine's short-lived marriage to Curly, my cousin Emily Trager felt that Elaine's parents and Jennie had much to do with their divorce. Another cause was the fact that Curly was rarely at home and Elaine was continually left alone. Emily also felt that Curly was sorry that he had divorced Elaine. Elaine, on the other hand, had quite different thoughts on the subject, and I was determined to learn more about her relationship with my uncle Curly and find out what finally caused them to split up.

In spite of past family friction, I have kept in touch with my aunt Elaine through the years and was delighted when she agreed to be interviewed on this touchy subject.

Elaine Ackerman Howard Diamond was born August 12, 1914, in Far Rockaway, New York. Her parents, Emma and Isadore Ackerman, moved to California sometime in the '20s, and her father opened a jewelry store. Elaine's education after high school included two years at UCLA. In 1937 she married Jerome "Curly" Howard, had a daughter, Marilyn, with him in 1938, and received her final divorce decree in 1941. Elaine married Moe Diamond in 1943, and in 1944 the two had a son, Michael. Elaine and Moe resided in the San Fernando Valley.

INTERVIEW

Courtesy of the subject

Elaine Ackerman Diamond

March 25, 1985

JOAN: I was too young to really know Curly's mother—my grandmother. What was Jennie like?

ELAINE: This was a very cold woman. I never really got to know her well either. We met for the first time about six months before Curly and I were married. Then we left on our honeymoon and, after that, for a personal appearance tour.

JOAN: What was Curly's father like?

ELAINE: Well, I liked him. He lived with me from the time Jennie died. Why they picked me, I don't know. We lived at the time on Highland in a rented house. It was very close to Moe's house. I guess it was because I had more room than your mother. Marilyn was a baby when Sol moved in with us, and he was shocked that I gave her bacon. My pediatrician had recommended it. Sol was very orthodox and very kosher, and he had a fit.

JOAN: It's funny that you should speak of my grandparents and bacon, because that is one of the only stories that I recall about my grandmother. I was about eight, and I was as anemic as any child can be—skinny too—and the doctor had me on a diet to get fat, and one of the foods was bacon. I recall the story to this day. I'd visit my grandmother and she'd always quiz me about what I had eaten that day, and when I answered, "A bacon sandwich—and mother made me put butter on it," I thought this very kosher lady would faint. She glared at my mother, and I knew that I had said something very wrong.

ELAINE: But I honestly tried to adhere to Sol's dietary rules. At one time—I'll never forget this as long as I live—we had to soak our dishes in the bathtub to make them kosher for Passover. And no one was able to use the tub for over a week.

JOAN: Did they put anything in the water?

ELAINE: I think . . . salt. I'm not sure.

JOAN: Did Sol read a lot?

ELAINE: I don't recall, but there was another thing that I resented about him—not necessarily about him but all people that believe in orthodoxy. I am not a religious person. I went to Sunday school. My mother wanted us to learn the history of the Jewish people, and after that we were on our own. We had very little religion in our home. I remember . . . Sol would get up about five in the morning and go to shul, and then again at five in the afternoon. In between he'd rant and rave that everybody—they should drop dead, they should burn in hell, things like that.

JOAN: People that he knew?

ELAINE: No—the help—because they used too much water. He would watch them like a hawk.

JOAN: It's funny that you mention this, because in one of my interviews with my father's niece, Bernice Herzog, when I mentioned that one of Sol's sisters worked in Jennie's house, she laughed hysterically and said, "That girl must have really suffered. You heard about the help that worked in the Horwitzes' house? Jennie and Sol screamed at them constantly." I wonder if Sol could have been getting senile.

ELAINE: I don't know. In later years, it bothered me to think that anybody so religious had to spend his days cursing.

JOAN: He was almost seventy then.

ELAINE: I'm not senile, and I'm seventy.

JOAN: Was Curly creative in his offscreen life?

ELAINE: Did you ever know that they told me that Curly was a child prodigy at the piano?

JOAN: I knew that he had a wonderful voice. It's possible that he played the piano. My cousin told me he worked as a song plugger, and usually song pluggers played the piano as they sang.

ELAINE: I remember that when Marilyn was growing up—after I was divorced—she wanted to take piano lessons, and I said to [my husband], "We've got to get a piano for her; she may be like her father." I don't know who told me about Curly's talent—his mother or

Shemp's wife, Babe. Marilyn had no talent at playing piano, but her son, Darren, seems to have picked up the musical gift, because he plays the piano extremely well. He graduated from San Francisco State, Phi Beta Kappa, cum laude in Drama and Musical Arts.

JOAN: What kind of career did you have?

ELAINE: I started in my early years at the May Company as a saleswoman, and then I went to college, and my first job was secretary to the comedian Joe Penner. After that, I got a job as a secretary to a well-known business manager for movie people. And then I started working at the place where I met Curly.

JOAN: How did you meet Curly?

ELAINE: That's a very funny story. At that time, I worked for a wholesale furrier on Los Angeles Street, downtown. I was a model and also worked in the office. I remember . . . everybody wanted to fix me up with their friends. One day your grandfather, Sol Horwitz, came in, and when he left, my boss said to me, "This man has a son who is one of the Three Stooges." At that time, I'd never heard of the Stooges. I was not into comedy or anything like that. My boss said they were very well-known comedians and that Mr. Horwitz would like me to meet his son. I told him I was really not interested. The next day, as I was ready to leave for lunch, in comes Curly Howard. I was introduced to him, and then I left for lunch. When I came back, he was still there, and he didn't know what to say. He was rather shy with me. He finally said, "Did you have a good lunch?" And I said, "Yes, thank you." And I went back about my business. Well, the next thing that happened—this is really a coincidence—that evening, a doctor that I had dated before called; he was staying at the Ambassador Hotel. He had no car, and the first time we went out, my mother let us take her car. This was the same night as the day I had met Curly—and I get a call from this doctor, and he asks me out for dinner. This time I suggested we take a cab. I didn't want to ask my mother for the car again. He told me he didn't need a car, as he had just made friends with someone at the bar and we were going to double date with him, and he had a car. I don't know what made me ask, but I said, "What's his name?" Then he said, "Well, he's one of the Three Stooges. His name is Curly Howard." I said, "Well, you tell Mr. Howard that I'm the girl that works for Morty Mandel, and I met him today." Well, that was like an omen to Curly. He got on the phone and told me that they would pick me up. And that was the beginning of the romance.

JOAN: What an unusual story. I guess truth is stranger than fiction.

ELAINE: He swept me off my feet. He seemed to think it was meant to be. To meet twice in one day—and such different circumstances.

JOAN: And to have his father play cupid!

ELAINE: After that, I honestly didn't know what hit me.

JOAN: How old were you?

ELAINE: I wasn't that young. I was about twenty-two. We didn't go together long. We got married the next year. [Pause.] I just thought of another very interesting story, one that occurred when we were engaged. Curly gave me a lovely ring that he got from my father, who was in the jewelry business. It was a beautiful diamond. This was about a week before we were to be married. He explained that he had to supply the liquor for the wedding. He told me he was going to pick me up and go to the Ambassador to see about the liquor, and I told him that I had a friend who lived nearby and that I would visit her and then come back to pick him up. I went to my friend's house but she wasn't in. And right in the next block was [Dr. Mueller], our family doctor. While I was engaged, I used to take Curly's mother there. As I drove up the street, I realized that this was the street where the doctor's office was. I said to myself—like I had ESP—"If I see Curly coming out of that doctor's office, I'll know that there's something terribly wrong." And at that very moment, I see Curly coming out. Well, I was just in shock. When he came over to the car I threw the ring at him and said the wedding was off, that I couldn't trust anybody that lies. How could he tell me he was going to the Ambassador when he was going to the doctor? I didn't want to hear—I was just hysterical and insisted he take me home. He left me and went over to your folks' house. They called me and begged me to let them explain. It was a very peculiar story, and I don't recall all the details. But I remember the main reason—if it's true. Curly said he had a wart on his penis and had to have it removed. Finally, he said, "If you don't believe me, I'll show you." And he starts to unzip his pants, and I was a naive girl in those days and a virgin—there were such things, you know—so I said never mind. I didn't want to see a bandaged penis.

JOAN: Was Curly fun? Some people have said he could be dull.

ELAINE: Well, he was fun. Especially when he'd get drunk.

JOAN: Do you think he was an alcoholic?

ELAINE: I don't know. He never drank during the day, but occasionally I'd smell alcohol on his breath when he'd come home from the studio, and he'd say he'd had a beer. But at times when we'd go out—I can remember on the personal appearance tours—he'd get pretty high when we'd be in a nightclub. He'd take the tablecloth and pull it off and rip the fabric to the beat of the music. It was beautifully done—and the spoons, he played them very well. And, of course, the tablecloth was always on our bill.

JOAN: Did he like to dance?

ELAINE: I think he was a very talented man. He was very light on his feet. I was never very much into dancing. I was not a good dancer, and I don't recall dancing with him. I must have, but I don't recall.

JOAN: Did you ever see him read a book?

ELAINE: No, I don't think I did. We didn't have television. But he would study his scripts. It was such a short time that we were married, and most of that time he was either making movies or was on personal appearance tours. I really didn't get to know him that well. And then the Stooges went to Europe.

JOAN: Yes, I was twelve when our father, Curly, and Larry went on a personal appearance tour of England, Ireland, and Scotland. [Pause.] Can you recall any interesting stories—funny or sad—that happened then or at any other time during your marriage to Curly?

ELAINE: [Pause.] There was one funny story. Curly and I were living on Edinburgh Street in Hollywood. I remember having a party, and Curly said I could invite all my friends. My friends and his friends were so entirely different. He didn't have very many friends that I knew of—all associates from business. Anyway, we had this party, and the theme was gambling. Curly was quite a gambler. That was another thing we did a lot of. We'd go to ball games on which he'd gamble. He loved that—and the fights at the Hollywood Legion on Friday nights. So he put this Las Vegas night together with all my friends—whom I never saw again after that night. We played roulette and craps, and he took all their money—not intentionally, but the house always wins. [Pause.] I can't recall any other funny situations. Most of my life with him wasn't that funny—even the honeymoon. Curly took me to this dude ranch near Reno. I spent my whole honeymoon on horseback—and I hate horses.

JOAN: Then he liked horses?

ELAINE: I don't think so.

JOAN: How did Curly feel about becoming a father?

ELAINE: I remember that Marilyn was born prematurely—and we were living in a house we were renting in Beverly Hills on Maple Drive. I don't recall how he felt. He was away most of my married life. [Pause.] I remember one instance—before I had Marilyn. He had this dog. It must have been the dog your father gave us, and it had puppies. I remember getting in the car and driving all the way to Columbia Ranch in the Valley—where he was making a short—to tell him the puppies were born, and he was so thrilled. He really loved dogs.

JOAN: Wasn't there any nightlife? After all, these were the golden years in Hollywood.

ELAINE: I don't recall too much about what we did at night. I know he did a lot of running around. I was usually not included, and eventually I got very jealous of it.

JOAN: Did you enjoy touring with the Stooges?

Elaine with Curly's first daughter, Marilyn (1938).

Courtesy of Elaine Howard Diamond

ELAINE: Curly wouldn't let me near the theater. It was a horrible experience. He just didn't want me to be in that atmosphere. I have a feeling that he put me somewhat on a pedestal because of my background—my parents.

JOAN: There are some men that treat their wives this way.

ELAINE: Well, sex was not so good with him. I remember once on a trip—an overnight trip—he was just awful because some man started to talk to me. And it happened to me several times when we were in a bar. If anybody started to talk to me he'd say, "Get upstairs." He apparently was very jealous, and there was no reason to be, because I never looked at anybody else.

JOAN: Irma Leveton, my mother's closest friend, once said, "I can't imagine Curly saying 'I love you' to any woman."

ELAINE: No, I can't either. But apparently this pedestal he had me on kept our sex life quite poor. And of course this was my first experience. In those days we didn't talk about sex.

JOAN: I'm sure Curly had had quite a bit of experience with women.

ELAINE: He was married before, you know. For a while they told me that the marriage was annulled. When Marilyn was born, I thought I had an illegitimate child and had my cousin, who was assistant district attorney in New York, check on it. I had to find out if I was legally married.

JOAN: I'd love to know where Curly married his first wife.

ELAINE: It was in New York, because they looked it up. It was registered as a divorce.

JOAN: How do you feel about mentioning that you were married to Curly?

ELAINE: I love it. I get a kick out of it. At work they—the kids who are now in their twenties—still watch Curly on Saturdays.

JOAN: Do you ever watch the comedies?

ELAINE: Once in a great while. Moe [my husband] will turn it on and say, "Come quick, Curly's on." The first time that I ever saw the Stooges' stage show was on my first personal appearance tour [with Curly]. I'll never forget it, Joanie. It was in Chicago. I was in the audience, and here I see Moe and Larry on the stage and your father poking Curly and slapping him and throwing pies in his face. I got so hysterical that they had to take me out of the theater.

JOAN: Hysterical laughing or crying?

ELAINE: Both. I couldn't believe that I was married to *that!* You know, once he had cherry pits taken out of his ears from the pies. He had an ear infection—and the doctor examined his ear and came out with a pit.

JOAN: If you had it to do over again, would you have married Curly?

ELAINE: Well, it wasn't the happiest time of my life. Another unhappy instance I remember occurred when the Stooges opened in *George White's Scandals*. I was still married to Curly, and Marilyn was a year old, and he wanted me to come to New York. I remember it clearly. He sent for me—I went by train—and when I got off the train, he was waiting for me, and as I put my arms around him he said, "When are you planning to go back?" That was the way he was. He wanted something very badly, and as soon as he got it, he was no longer interested in it. Not only me but many things.

JOAN: Look at the houses. He went from house to house, dog to dog, car to car. A restlessness.

ELAINE: When he asked me to leave after asking me to come to New York, it was an awful feeling. A lot of it was not the most wonderful, romantic first marriage.

JOAN: Was he a kind man?

ELAINE: Yes—usually—and he was very generous. I remember once he bought me two mink coats. I think they might have been hot.

JOAN: Did he have a temper?

ELAINE: Not really. He was very good to my parents. My sister said to me the other day, "You know that Curly was very good to [our] daddy. He used to take our father to the fights, ball games, was very patient and sweet to him."

JOAN: Did your parents like Curly?

ELAINE: Yes. But they objected to my marriage. They felt we were complete opposites. [Curly] always used double negatives in a conversation and, after all, I had gone to college. When we did break up, I tried in many ways to hold that marriage together. I went to a judge who had a reconciliation court in L.A., and I made lists of his [Curly's] background and mine and went downtown hoping that he could help us, but it didn't work. Several times I tried to go back to him after we were divorced. You have a little baby and you want her to have a father and have him share that. I think I even asked him once. He was the one that said no, that it wouldn't work. It was probably for the best, because had I been with him when he got sick, I would never have left him. And he did become ill soon after that.

JOAN: Some people have said that Curly used vulgar language.

ELAINE: I think that's maybe true, but around men—not around women. Today we do use that four-letter word, but I don't recall him ever using [vulgarities] around me.

JOAN: What were Curly's feelings about my father?

ELAINE: He had a very high regard for him. He idolized him. Anything that ever happened between us, he'd run to your father. I did the same thing—went to your father with my problems.

JOAN: Was Curly moody? Was his temper quick or slow?

ELAINE: I never recall him getting really mad. But I recall one time when I took our dog for a walk and he was accidentally killed. Neither of us ever said anything. But we both ran in different directions. I was scared of what he would do. I had no right taking the dog out. And he couldn't face the fact—or face seeing that dead dog. He just ran. We both wound up at your father's house, and that was when Moe gave us his little dog.

JOAN: You mentioned earlier living in Beverly Hills. When was that?

ELAINE: When Marilyn was a baby. We had a nurse, a chauffeur, and a maid who cooked— that's a lot of help. We lived in Beverly Hills on Maple in a beautiful house. The year was 1938.

JOAN: Was Curly a complainer or did he ignore his problems?

ELAINE: He didn't complain about his health. He didn't have any problems when I was married to him.

JOAN: Did liquor change Curly's personality?

ELAINE: Yes. Most people get happy when they drink. He got mean—very nasty. He'd push me around. He never hit me. I never saw him when he was that drunk, but he would slur his words and just get very belligerent.

JOAN: Did he ever seem sad?

ELAINE: The only time I saw him sad—he got stinking drunk—was when his mother died. I remember the Stooges were onstage, and when they came off, they were given a telegram. And instead of going up to his room—or being civil about it—he went with me to the hotel bar and proceeded to get extremely drunk.

JOAN: I feel he ran away from life.

ELAINE: Yes.

JOAN: Did his bad foot bother him a lot?

ELAINE: No. I recall seeing a big scar, and he would limp. I don't ever remember him complaining about it.

JOAN: Was Curly well liked?

ELAINE: Oh, yes. They all loved him as a celebrity. Wherever we went, they wanted autographs and pieces of his clothing. They did that to all the Stooges. When we went to Atlantic City and he walked with me down the Boardwalk, he'd come home with half his suit missing.

JOAN: Do you feel the divorce affected Marilyn any way?

ELAINE: The only thing that I felt badly about is that she didn't get to know Curly at all. She knew him only after he had those strokes, and she—the few times I brought her over there—she was afraid of him because he was so ill. Before that, when he was feeling better, he'd come to visit at our house and—after all, she was older by then—he'd bring her a little toy that was appropriate for a baby—a stuffed bear or a stuffed dog—so she didn't appreciate the gifts he brought her. But he was very good-natured about it.

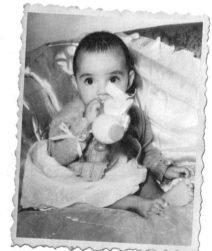

Curly and Elaine's daughter, Marilyn, at the age of one. What incredible eyes! (1939)

Courtesy of Elaine Howard Diamond

I completed my taping of Elaine's interview at her lovely Valley apartment. We kissed good-bye, and I realized that this book on Curly was becoming a catalyst that was bringing my family together again.

Curly poses for a family photo. Back row, left to right: Clarice Seiden, Moe's sister-in-law; Curly; and Elaine. Front row, left to right: Bill Seiden, Clarice's son; the author; and Shemp's son, Mort (1938).

Sheet music from the famous Stooges "Alphabet Song" from *Violent Is the Word for Curly* (1938).

Publicity still from *Flat Foot Stooges* (Columbia, 1938).

Curly gives his customer a "pet-icure" in *Mutts to You* (1938).

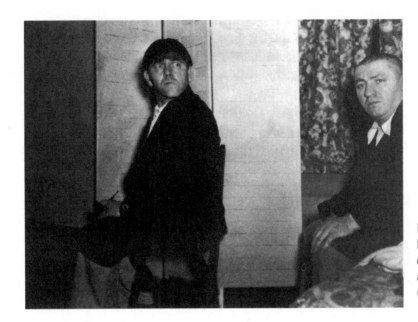

Moe and Curly backstage in a dressing room at Columbia (1938).

Reminiscing about Curly with Elaine refreshed my memory about other humorous stories that my father had told me of their trip to Europe. In the spring of 1939, the Stooges signed a contract for an extended vaudeville tour of England and its provinces, including a two-week stint at the famous London Palladium.

Several weeks before his departure on the *Queen Mary*, Curly was worried about being a poor sailor and told Moe of his fear of getting seasick. Moe, who had done a lot of fishing in Sheepshead Bay, reassured Curly, insisting that he come out for a ride with him in the bay. They'd rent a rowboat and he'd get used to the water. For good measure, Moe would test an old seaman's formula he had heard about and would wrap Curly in wet newspapers. Curly thought he was nuts and refused. Their rowboat ride went without incident, and Curly was positive the wet-newspaper bit was an old wives' tale. Once aboard the *Queen Mary*, amidst the pitching and rolling of the high seas, Curly got violently ill. He raced throughout the ship, collecting newspapers, wetting them, and wrapping himself up like a fat mummy. But the old seaman's cure was either ineffective or too late, and his nausea continued sporadically throughout most of the Atlantic crossing.

When the boat docked in England, Curly was amazed at their fabulous reception. He never realized that their films had preceded them for the past five years and that their British fans were legion. A few days later, in a scene reminiscent of Atlantic City and Curly's problem with youthful fans, a group of pink-cheeked London lads leaped onto Curly and, before he knew what was happening, tore the pockets from his coat, grabbed his hat, and dashed off with their Curly souvenirs.

It is interesting to note that in the Irish language the word *stooge* is a slang term for intercourse, and throughout Ireland the boys were billed as the Three Hooges.

The tour was extremely successful, despite the fact that World War II began while they were in England and the entire country went on a wartime footing. The Stooges returned to the States

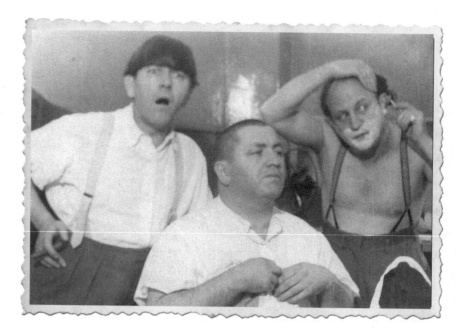

Moe, Curly, and Larry in the dressing room, getting ready (1939).

Curly at the Dublin, Ireland, zoo with a feathered and nonfeathered friend (1939).

Moe, Larry, and Curly with fans on their tour of England (1939).

on the *Queen Mary's* last voyage before being converted to a troop ship. Immediately upon their arrival in New York, they started rehearsals for the Broadway musical *George White's Scandals*.

During the run of the *Scandals*, I can recall watching the show from the wings. There is nothing more exciting to me in the theater than viewing the performers from that space at the side of the stage between the wing and the act curtain. It always ran through my mind that if someone accidentally pushed me, I could be onstage—looking out at that frightening sea of faces with mixed feelings of both fright and delight. My uncle Curly was a pro, and he often told me that even he would get butterflies in his stomach at every performance until he knew the audience was with him.

As I watched Curly rehearsing onstage in 1939 for *George White's Scandals*, I was able to see closely his cute, crooked, toothy grin when my father treated him sweetly and the sharp, comical contrast when Moe slapped him about; Curly's mouth would open into a little circle, his brows would raise, and that funny mad-little-boy look would come over his face. Oftentimes, Curly's inventive sounds and original mannerisms were used by him to cover up an inability to remember his lines. This was especially so in the Stooges' films, where even his famous "woo-woo-woo" was created to cover up his memory lapses. In the *Scandals* there was a point in the act where the Stooges would each do a comical dance step, and Curly's choice was always the shoulder-spin, which he executed on a filthy, splinter-ridden wooden stage, often getting a sliver or two in his ample buttocks. There are, to this day, many who believe that Curly was the original inventor of break-dancing.

This Columbia still photograph captures Curly during filming of *Three Sappy People* (Columbia, 1939).

Curly, with his faithful Havana cigar, poses with the other two Stooges for a publicity still for an installment of *Screen Snapshots*, a series of documentary shorts produced by Columbia (1939).

Portrait of Curly's father, Solomon Horwitz (1939).

The Three Stooges mimic their three puppets (1939).

On this particular opening night, the Stooges walked slowly up to center stage dressed in the darnedest, crummiest conglomeration of formal dress imaginable: grey pin-striped pants; ill-fitting black frock coats; yellow, wrinkled, perspiration-soaked dress shirts; goofy black plastic bow ties; and funny little low boots called "congress gaiters." Larry and Moe's wardrobe fit sloppy-loose, while Curly's fit him like a second skin stretched tightly over his chubby body. I was in the wings and probably more nervous than either my father or Curly. When Moe belted him with the flat of his palm, the slap resounded throughout the theater. Saliva flew out of Curly's mouth, and I winced while the audience roared with infectious laughter.

The Stooges' comedy routines onstage had a delightful touch of the corny that, because of the magic of Curly and the indefinable chemistry of their threesome act, would never fail to delight audiences throughout the world. The Stooges' corn was plentiful. When my father would ask Curly what his occupation was, Curly would grin boyishly and answer, "I'm a tailor—and I can make you a beautiful suit with two pairs of pants and a belt in the back, including a vest, for *only* $675." Moe would reply scornfully, "Six hundred seventy-five dollars! You're no *tailor*, you're a *robber!*" Curly would quickly retort in his cute falsetto, "That's me, *Robber Tailor!*" At which point the audience would roar. Then Moe, as a topper, would give him a resounding slap in the face or his traditional two-finger poke in the eyes.

Whether on stage or screen, Curly's performance never ceased to amaze me. For a man of his size, he had the indescribable grace of a ballet dancer. When frustrated by Moe's face slaps and eye pokes, he'd stand on his tippy-toes, staring eyeball to eyeball at his glaring brother, and he'd vibrate his arms like the flippers on a paranoid penguin. Then he'd mince about with his hands on his hips and, like a frustrated little kid, speak in the most ungodly high-pitched squeak, a voice that seemed incongruous coming from the mouth of a grown man Curly's size.

On September 6, 1939, when the Stooges were a week into their stint for George White, Curly and Moe received word of their mother's death. The two brothers were shocked at the news and deeply mourned her passing. Their only consolation was the fact that they had kept a major family secret from her. Jennie's death saved her the grief of finding out that the apple of her eye—her first-born son, Irving—had died three weeks before her.

But in the tradition of all performers, the Stooges knew the show must go on. And although the show did go on, Curly was beside himself, because he was unable to go to his mother's funeral. The *Scandals* had a successful Broadway run, but Moe, Larry, and Curly were forced to leave the show before it closed and return to California to resume filming their shorts for Columbia.

Jennie and Sol proudly displaying a picture of their first son, Irving.

As usual, the Stooges took the train from Grand Central Station, and their departure was covered by the press. The following is an excerpt from a clipping found tucked away in my mother's old yellowed scrapbook:

There was a knot of little boys on the chilly, station platform. "That one's Curly," one of them said importantly. Another saw a pal across the platform. He whistled shrilly and jerked his head with the old "come here" signal. The distant kid broke into a loping run. "Hi, Curly!" chirped the bigger one. "How about your autograph?" Curly was glad to oblige.

The kids stood around while the Stooges spoke to reporters. "Why aren't they funny like they are in the movies," one youngster asked. "Hey! What's your dog's name, Curly?" shrilled another kid. "Shorty," said Curly succinctly.

Jennie Horwitz in Lakewood, New Jersey, in 1932.

With that Curly went to a newsstand to buy Shorty a paper to read for Shorty is a miniature schnauzer 5½ months old and such immature pooches are fond of newspapers for some reason.

Curly and Moe pose for newspaper photographers in Fall River, Massachusetts, with Curly's newest dog, "Shorty" (1939).

Back in Hollywood for another forty weeks of filming, Curly went straight to the cemetery in Whittier, California, to visit his mother's grave.

It is difficult to reconstruct how Curly felt at this point in his life. Moe once told me a story regarding Curly's answer to a reporter who asked him how he felt about the loss of his mother. Apparently, Curly had been asked the same question many times previously and had his answer prepared. He reached into his pocket, pulled out a torn page from a magazine, and read: "One day as I sat musing, sad and lonely without a friend, a voice came to me from out of the gloom saying, 'Cheer up. Things could be worse.' So I cheered up and sure enough—things got worse."

A few days later, the Stooges gave an interview where they reminisced about their trip to Europe and their visit to the Dublin Zoo. Whether said jokingly or not, Curly's words must have reflected his innermost feelings:

Larry to Moe, "Aw, it ain't so tough to be an animal. Think of the easy life they lead—no five shows a day, plenty of peanuts."

"But what about their short life span?" Moe interjected, "Think of that, my boy!"

"Who wants to live long anyway?" Curly parried.

This was late in 1939, and little did Curly realize that he would no longer be living a dozen short years from then.

5

THE '40s

Divorce and Short, Sweet Marriage #3 • Too Much Work, Wine, Women, and Song • He's Feeling Mighty Low • Marriage #4 and Daughter #2 • And a Stooge No More

In 1940 Curly's second wife, Elaine, separated from him and took their daughter, Marilyn, with her. Curly had mixed feelings about the instant loss of his family but shut his eyes and closed the door to that part of his life. To try to forget the aggravation of his impending divorce, he passed the time by spending his money as fast as he earned it, buying houses, dogs, and cars one after the other and giving in to all his whims.

It was during this period that several of Curly's male friends noticed a change come over him. A number of them remarked that he suddenly became very crude and vulgar, especially so when he drank too much—which was far too often.

Curly in the Columbia comedy *A Plumbing We Will Go* (1940).

Drinking? Carousing? I wanted to know more about this period in Curly's life, and I asked Dr. John Grenner, psychotherapist and dear family friend, if he would interview Art Seid, a film editor at Columbia who worked on the Stooges' comedies and was one of Curly's few close friends. The following is that interview:

ART: One thing I recall about Curly is his bad foot. The thing I visualize mostly is seeing this guy walking up the street—on Gower—dragging that foot behind him. He always seemed to be in great pain. I see it so vividly. And he always had some gal around him, and I remember this one time his carrying a little baby [Marilyn]. I also recall we got drunk a couple of times together.

DR. GRENNER: What kind of a man was Curly?

ART: The way I would describe him mostly, he seemed to be a very unhappy guy. There was a moroseness about him. Just like most clowns, he very rarely laughed. He worked very, very hard, as did all three of the Stooges. I kept seeing this unhappy man all by himself. We'd go out after work together, to a couple of saloons around Columbia—Brewer's, Brittingham's up the street. We'd meet, or I'd go down to the set. This was fifty years ago, and it's so hard to recall. I never knew any close personal friends that he had.

DR. GRENNER: How would you compare the Three Stooges—their personalities?

ART: Completely, completely different. Moe was very serious, very businesslike. He ran the whole show. Larry, I couldn't warm up to. Larry was a kvetch. Curly was the clown.

DR. GRENNER: A clown on the set?

ART: Once in a great while. Mostly, I would see him by himself. A loner. I think most of it was that he wasn't well. His leg used to drive him crazy.

DR. GRENNER: When you'd have a drink with Curly, did he talk about anything in particular?

ART: He didn't crack jokes. We were young guys. I was about twenty-one. [Curly would have been thirty-three.] He wasn't a high-energy person, and he didn't hang around very long. He'd have a couple of drinks and then go. We'd start out to make a night of it. Hollywood was a great place to be. We'd have a lot of fun. He liked to be with the guys, but he never contributed very much in the way of conversation. Then he just disappeared.

DR. GRENNER: When you went to bars, did he have a date with him?

ART: Not always when he was with me, but the other times there was always a girl with him. He was a real womanizer.

DR. GRENNER: Did the women—or others—have anything to say about him?

ART: Nobody ever put him down. He was a very hard worker. Dedicated. But Curly was a loner. As the years went by, I could see the pain on his face increasing. Even on the screen. I could see that the man wasn't well. He'd be dragging that foot. I could see it on the Moviola [editing machine]. Things just didn't work out well for him.

DR. GRENNER: Maybe it would be interesting to look at some of the old films and watch the changes in him. It would probably be during 1938–1941.

ART: Funny, being the trouper that he was, he never really stopped. Except that in his work they tried to give him easier things to do, because he was dragging his foot. They'd work out the routines so that he wouldn't be so stressed.

DR. GRENNER: Did he ever get sloppy drunk?

ART: No. He was a quiet guy pretty much all of the time. A loner. I keep seeing this same face. This lonely, unhappy guy.

DR. GRENNER: Can you draw me a picture of that face? Its expression?

ART: Well, it was sort of expressionless. Most of his expression was reflected in his eyes. I had a feeling that he had a premonition of some sort—of doom. I think that might have been in his head all the time. Anyway, he died young. He must have known that there was something wrong with him.

DR. GRENNER: Did he ever talk about his women?

ART: No. In fact, he never talked about anybody. He spent most of the time with us listening to everybody else.

DR. GRENNER: I heard that his language could be very vulgar. Was this true?

ART: Yes. But knowing the circumstances, you felt sorry for him. He had my sympathy. Like the scapegoat he played on-screen, who would always have the audience's compassion. Sometimes I'd want to wring his neck, but there was a boyish charm about him that was irresistible.

After concluding his interview with Seid, Dr. Grenner assured me that it had given him additional insight into Curly's personality and that it would be helpful for a later chapter, in which he would attempt to analyze my uncle.

Art Seid's words that Curly was a loner and had a premonition of doom dovetailed with all my memories of him during the early '40s, when I recall him killing himself with his late nights on the town. Totally exhausted the following day, he would have to force himself to go in front of the cameras. Each morning as the filming of the '40s shorts progressed, the pressures of his bachelor life began to take their toll.

It wasn't long before Curly's loneliness drove him to invite his nephew Norman Howard to come from Pittsburgh to keep him company. Norman recalled his visit with his uncle Babe in 1941 and said, "It was just great—we went everywhere together: to the Friday-night fights at the Hollywood Legion, fishing on the Santa Monica Pier, to Columbia Studio to watch the Stooges shoot, and when Moe moved into his new home in Toluca Lake, we joined in for the housewarming festivities."

Curly showing off his catch of the day, with nephew, Norman Howard, and current girlfriend. Santa Monica Pier (1941).

"Curly the Sailor Man" poses on the Santa Monica Pier (1941).

Norman Howard and his uncle Curly in Moe's garden (1941).

The Stooges pose on a Columbia set with Moe's nephew Norman Howard (1941).

The Three Brothers: Moe, Jack, and Curly (1941).

A summer's day at Moe's Toluca Lake home (1941). Left to right: Moe, Helen, Norman Howard, Grandpa Solomon, Paul Howard, Curly, and the author.

Curly and his father in the garden of one of
Curly's many California homes (1941).

"Say cheese, Sol." Moe and Curly with their dad (1941).

Curly with two of his fans on the Boardwalk in Atlantic City (1941).

A DAY ON THE SET OF *WHAT'S THE MATADOR?*

In 1941 Curly's nephew Norman Howard spent several days on the set during the filming of *What's the Matador?*, Curly's sixty-second short, which was released in 1942. Norman photographed the pictures that appear on these pages, with the exception of the one in which he appears.

What's the Matador?, originally titled *Run, Bull, Run!* (prod. no. 519), was directed by Jules White and written by Jack White and Saul Ward. This Three Stooges comedy was reworked, using stock footage, into the 1959 Joe Besser short *Sappy Bullfighters*. Scenes from this short were also used in the feature *Stop! Look! and Laugh!*

Curly, as in most of the Stooges' comedies, was the central character, forced by circumstances to play the hapless matador. In the plot, Curly charged happily into the bullring, convinced that the beast was a fake, with Larry and Moe inside a bull costume. As in real life, he was a "victim of soicumstances." Due to a mishap, he found himself face-to-face with a real bull. As always, the "victim" managed to overcome adversity. Curly charged headfirst into the ferocious beast, knocked him silly, and with shouts of "Ole!" was crowned Matador of the Century.

Behind the scenes, a pensive Curly takes a short walk (1941).

Jules White explains a scene to a very attentive Curly (1941).

La Señorita, Curly, and El Toro between takes on the set of *What's the Matador?* (1941).

Curly barks his approval of cousin Norman Howard, who warms up Jules White's director's chair (1941).

Finally, when Curly had to go on tour in November 1941, Norman returned to Pittsburgh. Curly was alone once again with only his final divorce papers and weekly child support payments to remind him of a family life that had gone awry. He didn't mind shelling out the money for child support—when he remembered to. What bothered him was the reminder each month that he had a daughter and that he had deserted her.

In 1942, upon his return from a Coca-Cola-sponsored tour of US Army camps, Curly found out that his cousin Emily was in town and asked her to stay with him. Emily hadn't seen Curly in years and found him greatly changed. He was no longer that sweet young boy, but in many other ways he was still the same old Curly. He drove a shiny luxury car, smoked the most expensive Havana cigars, and continued to suffer from loneliness.

When Emily returned from a shopping trip one day, she found Curly with several strange men seated around the dining room table, playing gin rummy. Puzzled, she watched and wondered why he was acting so peculiarly, constantly jumping up out of his seat after each hand, rushing to make phone calls, then returning to the card table with beads of perspiration on his brow. Sometimes he was smiling, more often he was scowling. When she finally asked him what was going on, Curly explained that he had staked several of his card-playing friends in other gin rummy games around town and was trying to find out whether he was winning or losing. Curly was a man of excesses; one card game, one dog, one house, one car, or one wife was never enough for him.

Emily also recalled that during her visit Curly had many lady friends, and she blushed when she recounted one particular incident that occurred during her stay with him. It was over the Passover holidays, and Curly received a beautifully wrapped box, a gift from one of his girlfriends. Emily stood behind him as he opened the package and was shocked to see it filled with marzipan cookies—every single one shaped like a penis. Curly had a good laugh. When I asked Emily if they ate any of them, she covered her face with her hands in embarrassment.

Bachelor Curly and one of his girlfriends (1941).

During the many months that I researched Curly's life in depth, I discovered that he had no trouble finding women. In fact, he had a way with them. A young reporter for a college newspaper, Phil Kaplansky, who met the Stooges in 1942 at the Palace Theatre in Columbus, Ohio, wrote to me about the first time he interviewed the Stooges. Phil had brought several friends along with him, two were women, and he was surprised to see Curly maneuvering one of the girls—a very attractive one—aside and asking her to dinner. The girl was a head taller than Curly, very chic, and the Midwest head of Collier Publications. She was a widow and seemed quite at ease with Curly and accepted his invitation. From what our young reporter learned from his lady friend at evening's end, Curly was immensely entertaining, telling her fascinating stories of his experiences with the Stooges, and that, all things considered, he was a perfect gentleman throughout the evening.

The following year, 1943, was not the most pleasant time for Curly. First, his brother Jack's wife, Laura, died. Shortly thereafter, on April 8, a Los Angeles County sheriff went to Columbia Pictures and picked up Curly's wages, which had been garnished. Moe, who always looked out for his kid brother's business affairs, was unaware that Curly was delinquent by thousands of dollars in child support payments.

But uncle Curly had his priorities. His money, as usual, went first for dogs, then for cars and new houses, and what was left over was squandered on gambling and nights on the town with his bevy of women friends.

My brother Paul and I will never forget the incredible variety of dogs that Curly had. We clearly recall cocker spaniels, high-strung miniature schnauzers, a big imposing boxer, and in the later years, his two collies, Lady and Salty. Some of them barked their brains out, some bit and snapped. All were one-man dogs and loved only Curly.

Man's best friend and his Curly (1944). (*left*)

One schnauzer, one Stooge, and one boxer. More of Curly's dogs during 1944. (*right*)

Curly, Shemp, and
Curly's boxer pup
(1944).

Curly mugging
with his
schnauzers
(1944).

In trying to explain Curly and his many dogs, my brother Paul said, "There was a definite connection between Curly and dogs and Curly and women; a woman was a complicated being, hard to understand, hard to please and to remain faithful to. A canine companion, on the other hand, made minimal demands, was always affectionate, cost very little money to care for, and was forever loyal."

Cars were definitely Curly's number-two priority. As long as I can remember, my uncle loved cars—the bigger, brighter, and newer the better. The one I recall best in the '40s was a bright, tomato-red Buick convertible, and oh, how he loved that car! Curly was an excellent driver and throughout his life could never understand why his phobia-ridden brother Shemp hated them so and had never driven in his life.

Besides his prized four-wheeled luxuries, Curly continued with his insatiable appetite for expensive cigars and high-style clothing. I recall him walking into our house in Toluca Lake one day brandishing an enormous cigar and dressed in an outfit that might be termed "early Liberace." He had on a green baize (a fabric resembling felt) jacket with pants to match, and draped over his shoulders was a stylish brown tweed coat. When my father saw him, he fingered one of the jacket's bright-green lapels, made a tut-tutting noise, and quipped, "So that's what happened to the pool table."

In between takes during filming of *Phony Express* (1943).

Curly's older daughter, Marilyn (lower right), at Paul Howard's
(upper left) birthday party in Moe's garden (1943).

On December 19, 1943, Curly's father Sol died, and a year that had commenced with unpleasantness also ended on a grievous note.

Curly bought another house in early 1944 and, still saddened over the loss of his mother, father, and brother—all in less than four years—asked his recently widowed brother Jack and nephew Norman to come from Pittsburgh to stay with him.

It was during this second visit to Curly's home and a later third, and final, visit that Norman got to know Curly really well, palling around with him, visiting the set, and taking photos of Curly, his dogs, and his girlfriends.

I telephoned my cousin Norman on February 18, 1984, and he was kind enough to take time out from his busy work schedule to allow me to interview him about his remembrances of his three stays with his uncle Curly.

Norman Howard, Curly's nephew and Jack Howard's son, practiced optometry in Redlands, a small town just west of Palm Springs. Norman had a wife, Ann, and two children, Robert and Judy. He was wild about dogs, a trait inherited from his uncle Curly, whom he visited in California from his hometown of Pittsburgh in 1941, again in 1944 when he was in the Marines, and finally in 1948. Among the many persons I interviewed, Norman was the only man alive who actually lived with Curly.

INTERVIEW

Courtesy of the subject

Dr. Norman Howard

JOAN: There have been various descriptions of Curly. Some have said he was quiet—almost dull—on the set. What was he like when you first visited with him in 1941?

NORMAN: Curly and the boys made three or four shorts during my first visit, and I spent most of the days with them. Curly was far from dull on the set. He'd play gin rummy and talk to the grips and with his director Jules White. When he spoke to Jules it was mostly about girls. Curly was single at this point in time. He was very open on the set and paid special attention to the female extras—especially if they were attractive. He eyed their scanty costumes, and Jules did his share of looking, too.

JOAN: Were people attracted to him—or was he a loner as some people have said?

NORMAN: When you ask if he was a loner, I would say just the opposite. As far as people being attracted to him, I feel he was quite popular. I remember the studio workmen—grips, electricians, etc.—who were on the set were very friendly and would shout, "Hiya, Curly! Hey, Curly!" You couldn't miss Curly with his round belly and shaved head.

JOAN: During your visits, did you feel Curly was an up person or a down person?

NORMAN: I don't recall him being depressed. There were times when his foot bothered him a lot. He shot himself in the foot when he was a kid, [and] he would emit several low Ooos when it bothered him, and he'd rub his ankle with Absorbine Jr. He couldn't lean over too well to rub it—because his tummy got in the way—and he'd ask me to rub it for him. I don't know if you'd call it pain, but it certainly was an annoyance to him. He was a heavy man with plenty of meat on his arms and legs, but the calf on this one leg was underdeveloped, and he had a decided limp.

JOAN: I have heard through several of Curly's male friends and associates that he could be quite vulgar in his speech. Do you ever recall him being like this around women?

NORMAN: He definitely curbed his language around the ladies and was very polite and attentive to the women he knew while I was in his company. He'd provide them with transportation. In fact, I recall driving several of his women friends who visited him on the set back to their homes. He was always kind and considerate to the ladies.

JOAN: What were the women like whom Curly dated during your visits with him?

NORMAN: They were pretty—not beautiful—and they genuinely liked him.

JOAN: What did you observe about Curly's moods?

NORMAN: He was an excitable type, but I never witnessed a real temper. He liked to have people around him. As I said before, he was kind and never abusive—that is, up until the time of his stroke. Afterward, I recall visiting him, and he was not the pleasant, fun-loving Curly I had known. But after all, he had had a stroke and never fully recovered.

JOAN: When was this?

NORMAN: It was before he married Valerie, and he had this girl living with him. The girl was very pretty and much taller than Curly. This was shortly after his stroke, and this girl was very attentive. I remember the contrast in his personality from my first visit. He seemed to be snarling and was emotionally unhappy about his state of health.

JOAN: You say his personality changed after his stroke?

NORMAN: Yes—he wasn't the same Curly. He was like a big kid in many ways. He would laugh about the most ridiculous things—the expulsion of gas was a source of humor to him. He would expel gas and say, "I can clear a room out." And it would tickle him so, he would break up. That was his boyish humor.

JOAN: [Embarrassed chuckle.] What were some of Curly's favorite things other than this?

NORMAN: He loved to play gin rummy a lot with the guys at a place on Gower Street—near the studio—and he usually was the big winner. He loved dogs and always had one. His tastes during my visits were for boxers and schnauzers. He also loved sports—especially watching the Hollywood Stars at Gilmore Stadium and the fights at the Hollywood Legion Stadium—and he loved women. Curly's conversations were usually about sports or women.

Jack Howard, Norman Howard, Moe Howard, and Curly Howard (1944).

JOAN: On one of your visits, Curly was between marriages. What were his relationships with women like during his bachelor days?

NORMAN: Well, Curly was footloose and fancy free. He was like a high school kid who had the wherewithal to do what he wanted to do. I remember one time—I was about eighteen—Curly and I and a friend of his were driving in his car, and the two guys were snickering because one had gotten the mother into bed and the other the daughter—in the same house—and each one was comparing notes and having a great time talking about it. Curly lived a fast life and enjoyed every minute of it. I don't think he had any regrets.

JOAN: Did you ever meet his last wife, Valerie?

NORMAN: I just met her briefly on a trip to California to take the optometry state board exams in 1948. They had this pool at their house, and I remember it was on Riverside Drive, and the freeway in later years went right through the property. I went over for a swim, and he was recuperating. That was why he bought the house with the pool, so he could use it for therapy. And, as I recall, Val was taking care of him.

Brother Jack, nephew Paul, sister-in-law Marie, Curly, and nephew Norman at Curly's home.

JOAN: Were there any earlier periods, before 1941, when you saw Curly?

NORMAN: I remember that when the Stooges were on their vaudeville tour in the late '30s, they would come to Pittsburgh, where I lived with my family. The first thing Curly would do is get in touch with a man by the name of Krugg, a theatrical reporter whose beat was the local shows. Krugg would fix him up with girls, and Curly would say to the stage manager, "Call up Krugg and let's get some broads." Or something to that effect. I was about twelve years old, and that was the first time I'd ever heard the word broad. As soon as he hit town it was "Where are the broads?" And women really enjoyed Curly. He knew how to show them a good time.

Curly stooging it up poolside with brother Jack.

Moe, Jack, and Curly.

My interview with my cousin Norman gave me a comprehensive man's view of Curly and has gone a long way in helping me to better understand my mysterious uncle.

By 1945 the excesses of Curly's lifestyle were catching up with him. His diet, which consisted mainly of greasy restaurant food and liquor consumed during his late nights on the town, resulted in his putting on weight at an alarming rate.

Smile! And they do: Moe, Helen, Paul, and Curly at Moe's home in 1944.

Curly, in shadow, with his then-current attractive lady friend.

On the set, Curly's performances were becoming erratic. According to director Edward Bernds, he did a fine job in *Three Little Pirates*, his next-to-last short, and was like his old self, but he was at his worst in *Monkey Businessmen*. Moe also noticed the changes in his brother, who was vibrant one day and sluggish and forgetful the next. Gravely concerned over these changes and signs of Curly's ill health, Moe made an appointment for him at a private hospital for a thorough physical examination.

On January 23, 1945, Curly checked into the Santa Barbara Cottage Hospital, where the doctor's report was frightening. He was diagnosed as having high blood pressure, malignant hypertension, a retinal hemorrhage, and obesity, and his EKG showed definite evidence of myocardial damage. The report panicked Moe, but Curly closed his mind to his medical problems. He left the hospital on February 9 and, at Moe's insistence, agreed to go to Palm Springs for a short rest before going to New York for a previously scheduled personal appearance.

In New York, Moe's concern for Curly's worsening condition became acute. He could sense the change in him from performance to performance. Curly's timing, vital to the Stooges' stage act, was way off, and each day his marvelous Curly mannerisms were becoming slower and slower. Moe was convinced that many of Curly's problems stemmed from his loneliness since his separation from his second wife, Elaine. He imagined how he himself might feel if he suddenly lost his family and home life and was determined to help Curly settle down. A zealous matchmaker, Moe soon discovered that the theater manager had a very attractive relative named Marion Buxbaum. Marion was a cute, petite blonde, and Moe, positive that she was Curly's type, arranged an introduction.

Curly and his brother Jack on the set of *Rockin' in the Rockies* (1945).

Curly being scalped by Moe as Larry looks on in Rockin' in the Rockies (1945).

Curly didn't need any pushing to get him to ask this chic, glamorous, elegantly groomed young woman to marry him. On October 17, 1945, after knowing her for only two weeks, Curly married Marion and acquired an instant family by becoming not only a husband but a stepfather to Marion's ten-year-old son by her previous marriage.

Anyone who knew Curly will tell you that he was a very generous man. All you had to do was admire something and he'd get it for you. It didn't take him long to spend a fortune on his new bride, buying her fur coats, expensive jewelry, and anything her little heart desired . . . which was plenty.

Back in California with Marion, Curly, anxious to please his new wife, purchased an expensive new home on Ledge Avenue in Toluca Lake around the corner from Moe.

Finally Curly had a home and family again, but it was not to last. From its very beginning, the marriage was stormy and wrought with problems. I was eighteen at the time and, as a UCLA coed with a new boyfriend, was too preoccupied to pay much attention to the rumors I had heard about Curly's growing marital problems.

Now, forty years later and desperate to learn more about Curly's third wife, Marion, I asked my brother Paul to share with me his recollections about her and her son Stephen. Paul searched his memory and wrote down his recollections.

The following is his letter:

In the mid-Forties, when I was ten years old, I became aware that Uncle Curly had married again. I didn't think too much about it except that I remembered his previous wife, Elaine, and his daughter, Marilyn, and I have the distinct impression that I liked them.

I can't remember a specific incident which led me to dislike this new wife, Marion, when I first met her. I know, however, that my group of buddies and I did not care for her son, Stephen. He was a sissified, super-refined, Eastern city kid, a wimpy-nerd of the Forties. I do remember, with some guilt now, that we used to tease him and refused to "hang out" with him, though I did see him from time to time at family dinners and we got along okay.

Marion had a sister, Irma, and I didn't care for her either. The two were always together. In my child's mind, they were evil and conspiring and I remember being afraid of both of them.

One afternoon, I was with my friend Tony Brand at his house, which was next door to uncle Curly's. We might have been teasing Stephen, maybe not. Whatever the incident was, Marion called to me, not in her angry voice, but in a calculatingly friendly tone, "Come here, Paul, I want to talk to you." I ran like hell into Tony's backyard and she followed me. Then I ran from Tony's yard into a vacant lot next door and she still followed. I climbed a wire fence separating the vacant lot from the street. I can see her now: me on the top of the fence and she, short and boxy with blonde hair and pale blue eyes, looking up at me. "Come down, Paul. I just want to talk."

I wouldn't come down and as I leaped from the top of the wire fence to the ground on the other side, my ring caught on the top of the fence and as it was forced off my finger, it removed a layer of skin—like the man in the deli carves a thin slice of smoked Nova Scotia salmon.

With my fear and anger about Marion and the pain of the injury, I ran home screaming and Mom tried to calm me. Since no one else was home and mother had not yet learned to drive, we had to walk the mile to the doctor's office.

The injury didn't take long to fix and on the way back we walked down Ledge [Avenue] past Curly's house.

In the distance, I could see Marion's gray Model-A Ford parked across the street. The "rumble seat" was open and as we got closer I could see that it was that "sissy" (son of the "Bitch") sitting next to—I couldn't believe it—my *buddy, Tony Brand.* The traitor! Just before we reached the car, the doors on both sides opened and the two sisters emerged and blocked our way. They said something like, "We've been waiting for you." Mom, trying to be brave and tough countered with, "You'd better let us by or you'll be in big trouble!" and then she shooed me aside.

In a flash, one sister grabbed Mother from the back while the other punched her in the face and stomach. I can remember my feelings: (These two lady-thugs were pounding on my mother, not like women do, but like longshoremen/strikers beating up a "scab").

As I watched in horror, I heard laughing and saw Stephen and Tony in the rumble seat, laughing, acting like they were watching a three-ring circus.

I ran from door to door, banging and screaming, "They're beating up my mother!" But not one person would take one step beyond their doormat to see what was going on. After about four vain attempts to get help, I ran back to the scene to find everyone gone but Mother. She was leaning against the car with her face in her hands. Lowering them, she revealed a red and swollen face, ravaged by the pummeling of those two bullies.

After that moment, I can't remember anything. It was like a movie "dissolve" to the next scene at [Tony's father] Judge Brand's house. A large group of people were gathered in the Brands' living room. I don't recall what was said, but the room-tone was that of serious murmuring. At that point, the clearest emotion of the whole event took place. Mother was sitting in a chair, crying quietly, and I was at her side. I must say that all during my youth and beyond, I had trouble displaying physical affection. Hugging and kissing was so difficult for me. Yet there I was (when the chips were down) holding on to her with both hands, hugging her and trying to comfort her.

I look back thirty-nine years later and feel only pity for the sisters. And I wonder what uncle Curly could possibly have seen in Marion. The tragedy is that he failed to see what kind of woman she was before he married her. Maybe that in itself says something sadly eloquent about Uncle Curly and his women.

My brother Paul's letter brought back long-forgotten memories of Curly's third wife. For reasons that I do not recall, I knew only a smattering of this incident between my mother and Marion until I read his letter. I was aware that Curly's marriage to Marion was a domestic nightmare and that after three devastating months, Marion and Curly separated on January 14, 1946, and Curly sued for divorce. There were even rumors that the judge at the divorce proceedings had determined that Marion was a gold digger and had ordered her to leave Los Angeles County.

Several of Curly's relatives and friends had little good to say about Marion. My cousin Dolly Sallin remembers meeting her and recalls that she was very pretty and dainty and all wrong for Curly. "This dainty little glamorous thing appeared in court and accused Curly of never bathing, which was totally untrue. Curly was fat but he was always immaculate. Marion lied—she was trying to get everything she could from him. The shame of it! It was all over the papers."

One of Curly's best friends, Irma Leveton, said, "Marion used to barricade herself in her room in order to get out of that marriage. The things she said made awful publicity. When she and Curly were in New York, he spent a fortune on her, and then when she gets to California, suddenly she can't stand him. The marriage was a disaster and heartbreaking for everyone concerned."

The following quote taken from Marion's court appearance was published in the *Los Angeles Times* on June 26, 1946, and was part of her testimony before superior court judge Arthur Crum: "He used filthy, vulgar and vile language, kept two vicious dogs. He shouted at waiters in cafes, pushed, struck and kicked me, put cigars out in the sink."

In the same courtroom transcript, Curly complained, "She refused to live with me. She wanted half of everything, called me bad names. I married her two weeks after meeting her and gave her $250 for clothes, $3,750 for a mink coat, an $850 wristwatch and a $2000 Tiffany bracelet."

Curly treated Marion like a queen, and within months, under California law, she wound up with half of their community property, including Curly's cherished new house, which he bought for her.

Curly's brother Jack and his second wife, Marie, recalled with sadness the day that Curly finally left Marion. Said Marie, "We came home from work and he was sitting outside his house, in his car, all his luggage piled around him."

After the divorce, Curly seemed to go straight downhill. His sister-in-law Marie, who along with her husband was living with Curly at the time, felt that the aggravation he went through during his marriage to Marion was definitely a factor in making him sicker. Three months after his separation from Marion, he had his first stroke and was barely able to walk.

My husband, Norman Maurer, recalled Curly's sad condition and inability to perform simple on-screen action when he visited the set in 1946 during the filming of one of the comedies. The scene he witnessed called for Curly to pop several pills into his mouth, and he just couldn't make his hand perform this simple task.

Several months after Norman's visit, Curly was hard at work on his ninety-seventh short, finishing the shooting of *Half-Wits Holiday*, a remake of *Hoi Polloi*, a clever, funny film that was the final curtain on the career of one of the great comics of his time. It was a hot, muggy day, the air was stifling on the soundstage, and Curly, sitting in Jules White's director's chair, was waiting to be called for his last scene of the day. Moe and Larry had finished their scene, and the assistant director was calling for Curly. When he failed to answer, Moe went to get him and found him slouched in a director's chair, his head dropped onto his chest, unable to

Marie and Jack Howard with Curly at his home.

Separated from Marion and less than a month away from his first stroke, Curly seems to be his old self.

speak, tears rolling down his cheeks. Moments later, both brothers were crying. Moe, never an affectionate man, bent over and kissed his brother's forehead, and immediately the thought entered his head that Curly must have suffered a stroke.

Moe was correct, and Curly, in need of special care, was taken to the Motion Picture Country House and Hospital, that marvelous medical facility in Calabasas for people in the entertainment profession.

The stroke, although severe, left Curly only partially paralyzed. He was able to speak, but his once-infectious boyish smile and facial expressions had changed noticeably.

Accustomed to high living, and with no salary coming in, Curly had difficulties making ends meet. Without waiting to be asked, Moe and Shemp took an equal share of their paychecks and gave them to Curly each week. Moe was shocked as well as touched when Larry insisted on participating. Larry was not family, but there was great love between him and all the Howard brothers, and throughout his life, Moe never forgot Larry's generous gesture.

Sometime in early 1947, Moe, encouraged by Curly's improvement and anxious to reassure him that he was getting better and might ultimately return to work, made arrangements for Curly to return to films in a very limited capacity. A cameo role was created for Curly in the film *Hold That Lion!* The scene was not scripted but ad-libbed on the set, as Moe was not certain that Curly would be able to perform. In the sequence, as it appeared on-screen, Curly was a train passenger. The fact that he wore a derby hat on his head and had a clothespin on his nose made it hard to recognize him. During the filming, in order to have as few distractions as possible, Moe refused to allow members of the cast on the set, and only the Stooges and the technicians needed for filming were there that day.

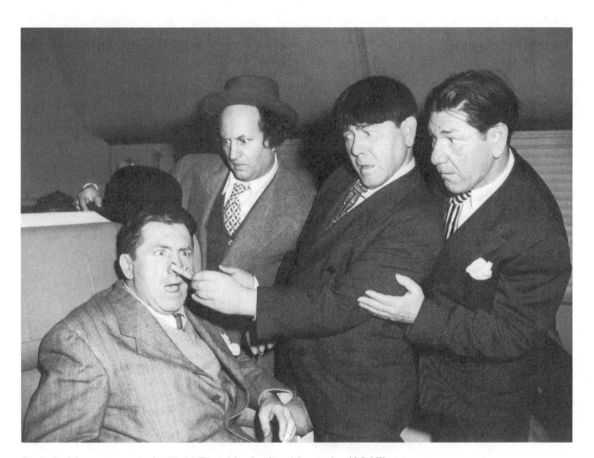

Curly in his cameo role in *Hold That Lion!*, after his stroke (1947).

Later in 1947, Curly was much improved and could finally get around on his own. The doctors warned him, however, that he must continue his diet, avoid liquor, and stop carousing.

Curly obeyed the first two of the doctor's orders but ignored the third. He refused to give up his nightlife, for that *was* his life, and continued to spend a great deal of time at Charlie Foy's Supper Club, a popular nightspot in the San Fernando Valley.

One night at Charlie Foy's, as the music blared and Curly was clacking his spoons, Foy came over to his table and introduced him to an attractive young lady named Valerie Newman. Explaining that Valerie's father was a longtime friend of his, he asked Curly to entertain the young lady.

Curly smiled and apologized to Val for not being able to join her for a drink, explaining that he was on a very rigid diet but he had an idea that he thought she might enjoy. Valerie grinned with delight at Curly's inventiveness when the waiter brought a chilled bottle of ginger ale served in a silver champagne bucket. This became a ritual for Curly and Val whenever they visited Foy's club, and during the next two months the two were inseparable.

On June 29, 1947, Curly left Val long enough to attend my wedding. This was a happy, festive event in the garden of our Toluca Lake home that must have given Curly ideas. One month later, on July 30, Curly married Valerie.

Curly's brother Jack and his wife, Marie, were living with Curly in his house when Curly and Valerie came home on their wedding day. They recalled how, without any advance warning, he barged in and introduced his new wife. Marie was piqued and taken aback. When I asked my aunt about her recollections of the event, she said, "He wasn't even dressed to get married. He and Val just went to the courthouse."

Curly getting the Stooge treatment from the Mills Brothers at a nightclub in 1948.

Curly after his first stroke, at the author's wedding in 1947, surrounded by his brothers Moe, Shemp, and Jack, friends, and Norman Maurer's father (left foreground).

Curly and Val's marriage license (1947).

Courtesy of Natalie Emery

A few days later, Jack and Marie moved out of Curly's place and Val moved in.

The remainder of the year was peaceful and happy for the newlyweds, and when Valerie told Curly in the spring of 1948 that she was expecting a child, he was overjoyed.

Val's sister Natalie and her husband, Tom Emery, had also married in 1947. Tom, a captain in the army, was stationed in San Francisco at the time and made frequent trips to Los Angeles with Natalie to visit Val and Curly. Tom remembered my uncle Babe with respect and admiration, as a man whom he described as a "kind, generous, and considerate gentleman." Those were his exact words and quite a contrast to the courtroom description of Curly by his third wife, Marion.

Tom also stressed Curly's generosity. When he needed a place to stay while his and Natalie's new home was being completed, Curly insisted that they live with him and Val. It was during this period that the Emerys and the Howards became very close.

In his desire to show me this other side of Curly's character, Tom related a story that he personally witnessed. On a drive with Tom one day, Curly spotted a young girl who was being pushed in a wheelchair and insisted that Tom stop the car so he could go talk with her. Caring and concerned, he asked the girl myriad questions: what she liked, what she needed, where she lived. When they left the young girl, Curly went shopping, bought everything that she needed, and sent it on to her with no card enclosed, as he wanted his gift to be anonymous.

All these warm words of Tom's brought to mind the warm words for Val by the members of my family and the many friends I recently interviewed. My uncle Jack's daughter, Dolly, had some glowing words to say: "I saw Val and Curly, and she was extremely kind to him, both solicitous and loving, and it never came across as anything but real. She was so different than the other women who moved in with him. She was a lady."

Moe and Helen's best friend, Irma Leveton, said, "She was one of the few decent things that happened to Curly and a woman who really seemed to care about him. Val and Curly used to

Valerie Howard (1947).
Courtesy of Natalie Emery

go to downtown Los Angeles with my husband, and he noticed that she genuinely cared about him. I recall she was with Curly twenty-four hours a day. When I visited him at the Motion Picture Country Home, she was always there."

And so, according to everyone who knew Curly and Val during this era, there grew out of their relationship a great mutual affection. Curly seemed happier than at any time in his life. He had no need to resort to wisecracks or vulgarities. He let his hair grow back and was finally able to be himself. No longer the immature Curly who needed to perform, he loved his new role of husband and father, and at last, in a loving home environment, his shattered ego began to heal.

On May 7, 1948, Valerie gave birth prematurely to Jane Cecile Howard, and for several days there was considerable doubt as to whether Janie would live. Thankfully, Janie survived and instantly became the center of Babe and Valerie's life.

Shortly after Janie's birth, Curly's health took another turn for the worse. He suffered a second stroke and was rushed to Cedars of Lebanon Hospital, where doctors at first felt that surgery on his spinal cord might help him walk again—but later, after further examinations, they decided against operating.

Upon his release from the hospital, Curly, although confined to a wheelchair, fought long and hard to get well so that he could be with Val and Janie, whom his life now revolved around.

Wanting to learn more of the details of this period in my uncle's life, I located Valerie's sister, Natalie, and after not speaking to her for over thirty-five years, I interviewed her on March 22, 1985.

Jack Howard and ex-Stooge Curly with a full
head of hair (1947).

Natalie Grenache Emery is the sister of Curly's fourth and last wife, Valerie, and aunt to Curly and Valerie's daughter, Janie. Natalie married Captain Tom Emery, who was based after the war at Ft. Mason, near San Francisco. Natalie and Valerie's father, Harry Grenache, owned Harry's Supreme Steak House, a very popular restaurant on Ventura Boulevard in the San Fernando Valley that was frequented in the '40s by many notables in the film industry, Curly Howard among them. Natalie and Tom had one child of their own—a daughter, Sharon—and raised Janie after Valerie died.

My interview with Natalie began as interviews usually do with a general query about my cousin Janie, whom I had not seen since she was an infant.

JOAN: Being Valerie's sister and having raised Janie after Val died, you would certainly be the best possible person to speak to about Curly and that period in his life when Janie was a child. What was Janie's childhood like?

NATALIE: Well, Janie led a very traumatic life as a young child. I didn't realize until the Stooges received their star [on Hollywood's Walk of Fame] that Janie's daddy was such a celebrity. To me Babe was Babe and Valerie was Valerie. They [the Hollywood Chamber of Commerce] invited Janie to go to the star [presentation]. She said she didn't want to go. She felt that it had nothing to do with her. This was for her father. It's funny, I never thought of Babe as a celebrity. He was just Babe. He was very different from what the rest of the world knew. We never looked at him as a star or as a sick man. He was a guy we all loved and was Janie's daddy.

JOAN: What about Curly and Val's married life? What do you recall?

Natalie Emery, Curly's sister-in-law and Valerie's sister, in Curly's pool (1947).
Courtesy of Natalie Emery

Valerie, Curly, Janie, and Harry Grenache, Janie's grandfather (1948).
Courtesy of Natalie Emery

NATALIE: Their marriage lasted about five years. Babe died, and Valerie got sick shortly thereafter, and my whole world changed. Tom and I, we had one child, and we ended up with the responsibility of Janie after Val died. But we never felt that Janie was a responsibility but just that we had the responsibility of doing a good job for Valerie and Babe's sake.

JOAN: How did you and Val feel about the entire Howard family—you know, the Howard brothers, the Hollywood scene, the celebrity world?

NATALIE: You know what people are like—everyone out to grab a piece of something. There was a great deal of love shared in your family. Moe was a good man, but he didn't know us from a hole in the head. He didn't know that we were really a bunch of very nice, weird people.

JOAN: Weird? Was Val weird?

NATALIE: My sister was a very artistic girl. Way back when people didn't care what was happening to the city [of Los Angeles] and one housing tract after another was going up . . . she started to cry. And when I asked her what she was crying about, she said, "They're cutting down the orange trees."

JOAN: If chopping down orange trees disturbed her, I can't help but wonder how she felt about her husband, Curly, being very sick?

Val, Curly, and bawling baby Janie (1948).
Courtesy of Natalie Emery

JANIE'S FAMILY ALBUM

All photos courtesy of Natalie Emery

Curly, Janie, and Valerie.

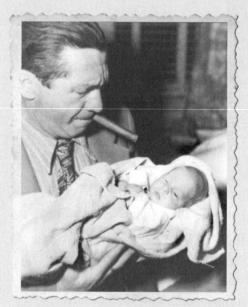

A proud papa with newborn baby Janie.

Curly, Janie, and Lady.

Janie with her new Curly haircut.

Like her famous
father, Janie lets
her hair grow.

A trim, slim Curly—no longer a movie star but still smiling (1947). *Courtesy of Natalie Emery*

Curly with cousin Dr. Milton Trager of the Trager Institute (1947). *Courtesy of Natalie Emery*

Curly with three of his favorite things: a lovely lady (his wife, Val), his dog Lady, and his new car (1947).

Courtesy of Natalie Emery

NATALIE: Val never saw Babe as a sick man. I never realized this until just recently, but Babe had a life [in show business] with everyone wanting a part of him. He was a very funny, great guy. Picture yourself as a celebrity—loved by all—being sick; people are afraid of seeing someone sick.

JOAN: But what about Curly, Val, and Janie? Tell me more about their personal relationship. You raised Janie? She was like your child.

NATALIE: Curly really loved that child. Babe would have loved a little boy, but when he had Janie, that went out the window, and their relationship was really something. No one was going to take care of his child. He didn't trust anybody.

JOAN: Was there a reason for that?

NATALIE: Janie was premature—a scary thing. She almost died. [My husband] Tom was in the service, and he'd come down from San Francisco and we'd babysit for Val and Curly so they could get away for a few days.

JOAN: Then Curly trusted only you to take care of Janie?

NATALIE: At that time, I was the only one. For me, taking care of Janie was never like taking care of a strange child. She was my baby, too.

JOAN: My father loved Curly, but I recall that after Curly died, my father drew away from Val and Janie. Do you remember anything about this?

NATALIE: Your father—he felt he was doing right. Your father was protecting himself and his family, and I'm sure if he could look down now, he wouldn't be saying, "I want to hurt Babe's child." I don't think he was that kind of man.

JOAN: Did my father's attitude affect Val's life after Curly died?

NATALIE: I have a family that I love, and I felt badly that Valerie had a very difficult life. But that's not your daddy's fault. I do think it was hard for Janie, never being accepted. But seeing the publicity on the star, it opened up her eyes that [Curly] was her daddy.

JOAN: How did Janie feel about her father being a Stooge?

NATALIE: You know, when Janie was a little kid, after Babe died, and she would see the comedies her father played in, she would yell and scream, hide her eyes. She didn't like that kind of violence, I guess. All these things must have been in this little mind of hers as she was growing up—the rejection, her father the celebrity. You don't talk in front of a child, but still they pick things up.

JOAN: You said "rejection." Do you mean my father's rejection?

NATALIE: I look at things now in a more open way, Joan. You shouldn't be ashamed of what your father did, because he didn't reject Janie to be a bad guy.

JOAN: He was very protective of Curly, but I think he meant well.

NATALIE: After you were pregnant, you gave me your maternity clothes and your father gave [my daughter] Sharon all her baby furniture. This was before Curly died. The minute Babe died, your father took Babe's body and had it sent to the cemetery [where Curly's mother and father were buried]. Valerie didn't even know where Babe was. It was obvious that Val was no longer considered part of the family. The minute Babe died, it was ta-ta. I don't mean for it to sound so terrible. But I'm sure that families get all mixed up trying to protect each other. Valerie was a very lovable person. Anyone who knew her could not help but love her.

JOAN: I don't remember Val that well, but I know how you must feel. I would like this book to be something that everyone in our family will be proud of—that after reading it we'll all understand Curly better—and I'm hoping that Janie and I will get a chance to meet each other and that Janie will finally get the opportunity to meet her half-sister, Marilyn, if she'd like to.

NATALIE: Joan, the only thing I care about is that Janie doesn't have any more [sorrow]. She's had enough. It really took a toll.

JOAN: What do you mean?

NATALIE: Janie was about thirteen when [her mother] died. When Val died she [Janie] didn't shed a tear. But she would wake up during the night and give out with bloodcurdling screams. I would take off, jet-propelled, to be there. And sometimes she would faint at school. People never knew these things. All they'd say is, "Janie didn't even cry."

JOAN: After Val died, did Janie live with you from that time on?

NATALIE: Yes, she did. But just before Val died, we were living in Washington, and Val was very ill, and they [Val, Janie, and Harry Grenache] came to live with Tom and me. Val actually started to become ill before Babe died, but at that time nobody knew anything about emphysema. She lived with us a while, and then Val, Janie, and my father went back to California.

JOAN: How old was Val when she died?

NATALIE: [Pause.] I must have a mental block. I don't know exactly—she must have been around forty.

JOAN: How did the family feel after she died?

NATALIE: I don't think anyone was aware of what went on in our life after Val died. Everything changed so quickly. It was like a nightmare—everyone dying.

JOAN: Natalie, I'm interviewing you in an attempt to paint a picture of that era in Curly's life—and Janie's—and do it with truth and honesty. I feel as though—on behalf of my father—I'd like to make up for some of the things that occurred, even though they were not done deliberately.

NATALIE: Regardless of what I've said about your father, I feel that this should put everything to rest. I'm no judge. The only one I feel badly about is Janie.

JOAN: Yes, let's put the past to rest. Let's make this book and Janie's share of the royalties a present from her father and my father.

NATALIE: [Starting to cry.] That's the part—I'm going to cry—that's the part that I know that Babe would have loved—to have left her something. He adored Janie. All I know is that the Babe I knew would have wanted her to have everything—but especially happiness in life.

After the interview with Natalie I realized that our conversation had brought back both good and bad memories for both of us and suggested that the balance of my interview be postponed until the following day.

The next day, before I asked my first question, Natalie apologized for breaking down the previous day. Natalie opened the conversation with:

NATALIE: I went back to Peter Pan land when I spoke to you yesterday. In my memories, I never really let Babe die, or Val die, or you grow up. Somehow, I always felt very responsible for Janie. I never let her grow up. She has always been "Baby Janie"—my responsibility. I felt I had to do a good job representing her mother and dad. Poor Joan, you got caught up in it all. I should have been on the couch, and [you should have] charged by the hour.

JOAN: I know how you must feel. I've felt the same way at times. I remember we left off talking about Janie. Did any other relatives besides you care for Janie?

NATALIE: Yes. My father put his all into Janie. My mother died shortly after Babe and Val got married. Then I married, and I lived with my dad for a short time. When Janie came into the world . . . it changed all our lives. And my dad turned out to be a sort of a "nanny." He moved in with Val and Babe and took care of Janie from time to time. Babe was not always well and had to go on a special salt-free diet. My dad, when needed, played a very important part in Val, Babe, and Janie's lives. His being there kept us all together.

JOAN: What were Babe's feelings about Janie?

NATALIE: Janie was very important to Babe. She was the little sunshine in his life. Babe didn't want any outsiders taking care of her and spent most of his time with her. He treated her as though she were made of glass.

JOAN: On Curly and Val's marriage license it says Val's occupation was a hostess. I had heard Val was a nurse. Was Val a nurse, or did she just nurse Curly when he was ill?

NATALIE: She did work as a nurse's aide at one time, and also she had a scholarship at the Art Institute of Los Angeles. It bugs me—that if you say someone is a hostess, it sounds so uneducated. I would hate to have anybody think of her in that way.

JOAN: What was her background, her education? Was she a college graduate?

NATALIE: Val went to Los Angeles Junior College and to UCLA for a while. I think she graduated from business school and received a scholarship from the Los Angeles Art Institute. She was a very creative girl.

JOAN: You said Val died of emphysema?

NATALIE: She had suffered from this disease for a long time. For years she didn't know she had it. It sounds gruesome to say this, but the doctors seemed to be thrilled—it was as though they'd found a new disease.

JOAN: How many years after Curly died did Val die?

NATALIE: Janie was only twelve when Val died. Janie was about three when Curly died—which makes it about nine years later.

JOAN: Did Curly seem happy during his marriage to Val?

NATALIE: I'm happy to say that he was. He would go back to the hospital periodically, but those were five very happy years. Tom [my husband] and I lived in San Francisco, and I would fly down to see Val and Curly. I recall I used to belly flop into the pool, and Babe, who would be sitting there, would say, "Gee, that was pretty good, Nat."

JOAN: Some people have said Curly was dull. Did he appear this way to you?

NATALIE: Babe was a very up person. He kept himself busy and never moped around. I really didn't know this other feller—the on-screen Curly. This man that I knew would come out with funny stories or something very witty and was always good company. It was remarkable. Babe lived his life as this nice person and didn't cry over the fact that he was no longer "Curly" the movie star who did all those slapstick crazies. He never talked about missing that other life and seemed to take it all in stride.

JOAN: Can you recall the time toward the end when Curly was really seriously ill?

NATALIE: I remember one time when he was in the hospital. We suspected he was having more strokes, because he would periodically get worse. This was a time shortly before he died. Your dad and mom were there, and Babe was having this terrible time trying to speak and make himself understood. He was trying desperately to say something. I imagine anyone watching us would think that we were all these sad people standing over this man, trying to find out what this important message was that this dying man was trying to relate. And then you would have heard all of us start to laugh and wondered what had gotten into this crazy group. We finally understood what Babe was trying to say. He wanted a dish of ice cream. It's strange; you see people in hospitals and you think they'd be better off dead. But after a time you realize that one time you could cry for them—it's so sad—and the next time you realize that their life does have meaning and they are thinking about the everyday things of life—Is the garden going to come up? Oh boy, does that kid of mine have a temper!—all the funny things in life and hearing their laughter.

JOAN: Do you recall any interesting, happy stories about Val, Janie, and Curly?

NATALIE: Oh, yes. Right after my daughter was born, Val, Babe, and Janie came up to San Francisco. Let me say—whatever Janie liked, Janie got. Well, we lived right by the marina, and there was a fellow with a pony, taking pictures. You paid him and he'd photograph your child astride the pony. Well, Janie had her picture taken and she didn't want to get off. Janie was spoiled, and Babe hated to see her unhappy, and he actually tried to buy the animal for her. Luckily, the man told Babe it wasn't for sale. Can you imagine bringing a pony home to our little apartment?

JOAN: How did Babe spend his days?

NATALIE: I recall one Christmas. I never saw anyone get as many neckties as Babe. I remember he was sitting in his chair with all those stupid neckties and laughing. Music was coming from the radio, and he had two spoons, clanking them together. He could play a tune with just two spoons and had people laughing all the time. There were times when he didn't have a lot to do, so just to make conversation, he'd call us his tax man and say jokingly, "If you want to get any money from me, you'd better have the government send me what it owes me."

JOAN: Did he ever get depressed?

NATALIE: I don't recall that. Anyway, he never made me feel depressed. He did like to do

Curly and his niece Jan Elliott (1949).

things in the garden. One time he was planting seeds and he stopped to tell me that I should appreciate being able to work. But he never seemed to live in the past and appreciated what he was doing at the moment.

JOAN: Did Curly ever speak about his work in the entertainment field?

NATALIE: I don't know if this would be of interest, but when Janie was little he would watch TV shows with her, like *Beany and Cecil*. One of the things that he discussed with me was the subject of comedy and where it comes from—where jokes come from and how many of the things that you watch that were childlike in *Beany and Cecil* were really great lines.

He wasn't just watching a little kids show, he was seeing the material and its relationship to comedy. I know who he thought was one of the greatest comics in show business—it was Jackie Gleason. He thought he was a genius.

JOAN: Did you ever see him read a book?

NATALIE: No—no. I don't really remember his reading. I really don't.

JOAN: Did Curly ever say anything derogatory about his mother?

NATALIE: No, he was very proud of her and her achievements. As a matter of fact, he said she made a great deal of money. He never spoke of his father.

JOAN: I wonder if Curly resented his mother.

Curly, still watching his weight (1947).

NATALIE: No. I never heard Babe say an unkind word about anybody or anything. Or even do anything unkind. I never met a kinder person in my life or a person who would be more willing to make you feel good. I thought he was a remarkable man. And he did love his brother. Babe and Moe loved one another very much.

JOAN: I think my father was more like a father to Babe.

NATALIE: I guess your father was. Well, he felt very responsible for Babe and watched out for him.

JOAN: My dad was a serious man. He didn't know how to enjoy himself like Curly.

NATALIE: That's true. I don't remember your father being jovial when he would come over to see Babe. Your mother—I liked your mother better than your father. But I think I understood your father—and your mother complemented him.

JOAN: Do you recall anyone else from the '40s?

NATALIE: Shemp used to come to the house. He was a very nervous man. I remember Babe would let Janie do anything to keep her happy. One day, she came down the back-porch steps in a pair of red high heels. She was three at the time. Ordinarily, if this happened today, I would fall over dead. When I was younger, nothing bothered me. But Shemp said, "My God, my God. Look at that kid. I can't look." I remember when he got in a car, he would hide in the backseat. Everything scared Shemp. But it's funny—even when Shemp was nervous, he was funny. You'd have to laugh at him. And Larry was fun, and he was funny. And I liked [Larry's wife] Mabel, although I only knew these people on the surface. And your father. I think I understood your father—and believe it or not, I never disliked him.

JOAN: Was Babe still crazy about dogs and cars in this era?

NATALIE: Yes. Val and Babe had two dogs, Salty and Lady, both collies.

JOAN: Do you think Janie has any desire to meet her half-sister Marilyn?

NATALIE: Well, I think you'd have to ask Janie that.

JOAN: What happened in Val's life after Curly died?

NATALIE: After Curly died? I felt very close to Janie. I adored her. Tom and I would come down to L.A., and whatever we would do, we'd take Janie with us. Then Val died, which was the time I was pregnant with another child, and I got a call—I knew that Val was not well, and I get this call that my dad died. And I went down to Los Angeles—pregnant. In a very short time, my baby died—at eight months. Her name was Kathleen. Then my father died, then Val. So that's why you'll have to bear with me.

JOAN: That was a traumatic period for you.

NATALIE: It sounds like everything was so terrible. I didn't have a terrible life. Even during the bad times, there were good times.

JOAN: Some people have said that Curly's language was vulgar at times. Did you find it so?

NATALIE: Movie people in those days—you know how they were. But right now—he would sound like Mary Poppins. He never used any vulgar words, but he did swear a bit—hell, damn. I really think, in all honesty, that Babe was a performer—a healthy performer. During his life in show business, he was very different as Curly.

JOAN: What did Curly do to keep busy during this difficult time?

NATALIE: Your dad used to come over and see him all the time. He loved your dad, and we'd go to your house periodically. His fans should know that there isn't anything to feel sad about. If someone could live the end of their life being ill as happy and content as Babe, it's not such a bad way to go.

(I felt drained, and Natalie must have as well, for she changed the subject and ended the conversation with the following:)

NATALIE: I want to tell you this, Joan, for whatever it's worth. Like you said, you don't have to do these things—write your book and include Janie and her half-sister. I'm sure you're doing what you think is right—and I really think I'd like to say [pause] thank you to you.

My interview with Natalie ended. It had enlightened me about many of the brighter moments of this difficult period in my uncle's life that I was never aware of. I felt much better with the realization that as the '40s drew to a close, Curly had finally led a tranquil existence as a husband and father, away from the violence of his life as the superstooge. He was, in his final years, satisfied to let his replacement, brother Shemp, take the blows and the bows. Finally, Uncle Curly was happy and content to stay at home with his wife, his little girl, and his dogs. He certainly had earned this bit of peace.

6

THE '50s

The End of a Comic Genius • Peace at Last • Curly's Daughters Speak

The fabulous '50s were hardly fabulous in the life of Curly "Babe" Howard. As the decade dawned, he was happily married and had a new daughter, whom he showered with love, but he was confined to a wheelchair. The heartache of being a shadow of his old vibrant, wild self was eased because of his surroundings and the constant attention of loving friends and family. His wife, Valerie, saw that he wanted for nothing, and visits from family members, business associates, and Moe, Shemp, and Larry eased some of the boredom of his confinement and enabled him, somehow, to survive and at times even enjoy this traumatic period of his life.

But love and affection weren't enough. Curly's condition continued to deteriorate, and Val, desperate to do everything possible for him, agreed with his brothers Moe, Shemp, and Jack that Curly would be better served if he was a patient at the Motion Picture Country House and Hospital in Calabasas, California.

On August 29, 1950, Curly was admitted to the Motion Picture Home for the second time. He spent several months there, where he underwent many tests and had the very best medical treatment available.

The medical care, the lovely country-like atmosphere, the constant visits by Val, Janie, and his brothers and their families, and being among other patients from show business seemed to improve his state of health. He was released from the hospital on November 15, 1950, and returned home.

During the following three months, Curly's condition once again began to deteriorate, and he was confined to his bed because of his paralysis. By late February 1951 he became so ill that it was almost impossible for Val to care for him properly by herself. Desirous of keeping him home among family and friends, she called the Motion Picture Home and requested a male nurse to help her. With his condition becoming worse with each passing day, caring for Curly at home and attempting to lead a normal family life for his benefit was more than Val could handle. Even with the help of a full-time male nurse, her plans were doomed to failure. No matter how hard she tried, nothing seemed to slow Curly's steady decline. He desperately needed the constant medical supervision that only a fully equipped hospital or nursing home could provide, and by the end of February, Valerie and Moe agreed that it would be in Curly's best interest if he was moved to the Colonial House, a nursing home in Los Angeles.

The following month, Curly suffered another stroke and his condition deteriorated rapidly. To make matters worse, the Colonial House nursing home was suddenly closed down by the City of Los Angeles when it failed to meet the city's fire regulations.

Curly was moved from the Colonial House to the North Hollywood Hospital and Sanitarium in April 1951. It was shortly after this that I visited my uncle and was shocked to see that he had become a mere shadow of his old self—a pitiful figure of what was once a vibrant and animated man. He could barely walk or talk. His wavy brown hair had grown back, and his rotund body had shrunk down to a dangerous level. The only sign that he understood what I said when I tried to speak with him were the tears that streamed down his face.

During his stay at the North Hollywood Hospital and Sanitarium, Curly conveyed to Moe his desire to have his collie, Lady, visit him. Months before, when Curly was at home, Lady always slept with him in his bed. Now that his health had reached such an alarming state, Lady refused to enter his hospital room and would only lie down in the doorway. One can only wonder why.

Finally, in December, the hospital supervisor advised the family that Curly was becoming a problem to members of the nursing staff due to his mental degeneration and would have to be moved. When the doctor suggested that Curly would be better off in a mental institution, Valerie was heartbroken, while Moe reacted vehemently. His baby brother would never, under any circumstances, be committed to a mental hospital.

Once again, Moe was left with the burden of placing his brother in a facility where he could receive the proper care. This time, after much research, the decision was made to send Curly to the Baldy View Sanitarium in San Gabriel, California.

Moe, Val, and the entire family now lived with a sense of dread, everyone waiting for the phone call they were certain would come.

Then, on January 18, 1952, the phone call came and their waiting ended. Jerome Curly Babe Howard was dead at age forty-eight.

Doing the research for this book, I realized that after more than thirty years since my uncle's untimely death, my long estrangement from Curly's two daughters was something that would have to be breached. Although I had spoken intermittently to Curly's older daughter, Marilyn, during the past several decades, I had not seen his younger daughter, Janie, since she was a one-year-old infant. Consequently, I was determined to contact both of them and put an end to this distant, almost nonexistent family relationship.

Since this book was about her famous father, I contacted Marilyn and asked her if she would be willing to participate in the preparation of the manuscript and share in the book's royalties. Her answer was in the affirmative, and we agreed to conduct an interview regarding her recollections of life with Curly.

Marilyn Howard Server Ellman was born in Los Angeles on December 18, 1938. Her mother, Elaine Ackerman, was Jerome "Curly" Howard's second wife, and Marilyn was Curly and Elaine's only child. Curly divorced Elaine after three years of marriage, and Marilyn, at age thirteen, was adopted by her stepfather, Moe Diamond. Marilyn went to North Hollywood High and upon graduating completed two years of college at

> ## Jerome Howard of Three Stooges Fame Succumbs
>
> Jerome (Curly) Howard, 46, of the famed Three Stooges, vaudeville and film trio, died yesterday at Baldy View Sanitarium of a long illness which followed a stroke in 1946.
>
> He leaves his widow, Mrs. Valerie Howard, and their daughter Janie, 3½; another daughter by a former marriage, Marilyn, 11, and two brothers, Moe and Shemp Howard. It was Shemp Howard who succeeded Jerome after illness forced retirement.
>
> Funeral services will be conducted tomorrow at 2 p.m. at Mallnow & Simons, 818 Venice Blvd., with interment at Home of Peace Cemetery.
>
> Born in Brooklyn Mr. Howard had lived in California for the past 20 years. The family home is at 11124 Riverside Drive, Toluca Lake.

Curly's obituary, January 18, 1952.

the University of Southern California. She married her first husband, Hal Server, in 1960 and had three children—Darren, Andrea, and Bradley. Marilyn and Hal were divorced after nine years of marriage, and in 1969 she married Mickey Ellman. After seven very happy years of marriage, Mickey died of pneumonia. Marilyn now worked at Micom Systems Inc. in the San Fernando Valley; her title, Supervisor—Component Purchasing.

On March 29, 1985, I had lunch with my cousin Marilyn in a bustling restaurant in the San Fernando Valley. It was the very first time that the two of us were able to sit down and really talk to one another, and it was thrilling to both of us that this book on Marilyn's father and my uncle Curly was bringing our family closer together after these many years.

I realize as I write this that Marilyn's recollections of her father are few, but the changes in her life brought about by her parents being divorced when she was only three are many.

The following is a transcript of my interview with Marilyn:

Joan Maurer; Elaine Ackerman, Curly's second wife; and Marilyn Ellman, Curly and Elaine's daughter (1983).

INTERVIEW

Courtesy of the subject

Marilyn Howard Server Ellman

JOAN: I realize you were only three when your parents divorced and fourteen when your father died, but what do you actually remember about Curly?

MARILYN: Mostly I remember toys—and stuffed animals. I don't remember him, per se. I remember him when he was ill. I recall that he was paralyzed: his wife waiting on him—shaving him. I don't recall the early days at all—period.

JOAN: Today, what happens when somebody finds out that your father is silly "Curly"?

MARILYN: When an older person finds out, they get so excited. It was never a big deal to me. I remember I usually hid the fact when I was young, because I didn't want to hurt the father I have now [Moe Diamond]. I was very concerned about that, because I adore him. Even my kids, when they'd say [their] grandfather is Curly, I'd hate it if they said it in front of my [step]father. I'd say, "Curly didn't do a goddamned thing for me as far as I was concerned." He was strictly a blood father. [My stepfather] Moe gave me the love, the attention, the money—the everything. He was a fabulous father, so I'd get very uptight if I thought he was going to get hurt. Curly wasn't a real father. He wasn't there when I needed him. He was probably dead at the time of my life when I would have needed him. I don't feel uptight about any of it now.

JOAN: Do you recall any things your mother told you about your father?

MARILYN: She told me he loved dogs, was an excellent dancer. She hated to travel on the road when they made personal appearances. I used to ask her, "Was he really funny?" She would say, "Well, he was normal." She always used to give me this thing [related to my weight]—"Watch out, or you're gonna die like your father." But I'm more like my mother. I get mad very quickly and I don't even know why. I'd yell at my kids and tell them they'd be grounded for the next hundred years, but I never followed through. When I look back, I realize I had a wonderful childhood. I adore my parents. I love my brother, but I don't always like him.

Curly and daughter Marilyn on one of her visits (1946).

JOAN: Do you miss not having known Curly?

MARILYN: I'm sorry I didn't know Curly better. I would have liked to. I don't think it [the divorce] was necessarily his fault. I think it just happened. Here I am making excuses for him. People have told me when I'd make excuses for others' faults—they'd say, "Don't be so nice."

JOAN: How do your kids feel about Curly?

MARILYN: My kids think it's great. They love show business. If Andrea [my daughter] had her choice, she'd be a singer. My son Darren's whole life is wrapped up in it—he acts and sings and dances and writes absolutely beautiful music. His father bought him Arthur Rubenstein's practice piano. It was thirty-five thousand dollars, and it's absolutely the most wonderful thing, and this kid drags it around wherever he goes—this grand piano, gold, inlaid inside, beautiful. He's played the piano since he was seven years old. You never had to tell him to practice. I put him in T-ball [pre–Little League]. He'd sit in the middle of the field waiting for the ball, but no kid of seven ever hit a ball out there. One day he came home and said, "I don't want to play baseball. I want to play piano." And he started to take lessons. It's his life now. He's written musicals. He writes the music and someone else writes the lyrics.

JOAN: Are the people at your workplace aware of who your father was?

MARILYN: After the star was set in the Walk of Fame, they put a little blurb in the company bulletin. I died! Nobody knew, and then I got so embarrassed. I'm fine with people on a one-to-one basis, but any more than that, forget it. I had to give a presentation in front of a whole roomful of people—managers and directors. I did it, but I thought I was gonna die. Darren can read [a script] cold. He must have gotten this from Curly's side of the family.

JOAN: When did you realize your father was a celebrity?

MARILYN: I really never thought about it. I didn't know my father was a movie star. I had no idea. The only time I realized it was when I was twelve years old and I saw him in the movies. Then I said to myself, "Oh, my father is a movie star." Before that he was only somebody who brought me a lot of toys.

JOAN: When you were a young girl and saw Curly sick, did you realize he was dying?

MARILYN: No . . . I just thought of it as frightening. Somebody that couldn't get up and play with me. Everything was done through Valerie [Curly's fourth wife]. It was very frightening more than anything else. I remember him—he couldn't talk, he couldn't do anything, he just drooled.

JOAN: Do you feel that you inherited any positive traits from your father?

Darren Server, Curly's grandson and Marilyn Ellman's son.
Courtesy of Marilyn Ellman

MARILYN: I have a feeling that he was a very good-natured, kind person, and that's what I feel I am. Sometimes it's not always good—believe me, it's not always good. I'm always making excuses for people. I don't know if I have his looks or anything. I have his build. Most people liked him, like most people like me. Not that they really know me deep down. It's more on a surface level. He really loved life, and I do, too. And I don't need drugs to help me with it. He [Curly] liked booze, is what I've heard.

JOAN: I discussed the subject of Curly drinking too much in my other books, but as more information comes in from my current interviews, I realize Curly would drink to relax after work or if he was very upset, but he never drank on the set or walked around smashed all day.

MARILYN: I don't think it was *accurate*—his drinking that much. I asked my mother. My mom likes a drink or two at night. I'm not like that. If I have a drink or two before dinner, there is no dinner—and no dishes. I get so relaxed I can't move. One or two drinks and that's the end of me. If I go past two, I'm absolutely bombed. I always have to be under control—that's the type of person I am.

JOAN: Do you recall what any other members of the family had to say about Curly?

MARILYN: I heard from Shemp and [his wife] Babe that he was really a good person. Even though he had his shticks. He was a good person. When I say he wasn't a good father, I think a lot of it has to do with my mother saying [to Curly], "I don't want to have anything to do with you. I have my life to lead and you have yours." I don't blame my mother, either. I look back at him and realize that he was my blood father and ask myself, "What did I get from him?" And I really don't know what I got from him, because I don't know what he was really like. And I read all this stuff [the books], and everyone is a little different. Shemp always said how great Curly was. Shemp said some really good things about him, and I was probably closest to Shemp. Shemp's wife, Babe, was a little bizarre. I didn't see the lunacy side of Shemp—he was so nice. He used to put me on his lap, real warm and real affectionate.

JOAN: My dad was not very affectionate. How were your parents when you were a child?

MARILYN: My mother is not very affectionate but I am, so I'm hoping I got that part from Curly. From my mother, I still only get a cheek.

JOAN: I do that to my sons, too; I give them a cheek. I hate to smear lipstick on them.

MARILYN: I think my brother helped make my parents more into a "today" person—they're opening up a lot more and saying "I love you." When I was a child, I don't recall my parents saying "I love you." I could feel love in the home, but I never remember them verbalizing it. I'm very verbal with my kids. I know it's because I missed the fact that my parents were not. I could honestly say, if it wasn't for my brother, my parents would be different today, still reserved. They were just that type. My brother said "f— you" all the time in the house, like the kids of his era. He wrote a paper on it. He brought a girl in the house for the first time and left a note on the outside of his door: "Do not disturb, I have a girl in here!" Would I ever do that when I was growing up? Forget it! That was the difference—those six years in our ages. [My stepfather] Moe is eighty-seven years old. My mom is eighteen years younger than my father. That's a big difference. Dad's from another generation, but he's so "cool" you can't believe it.

JOAN: My mother was like that. There was no generation gap between her and her grandchildren—or anyone in the family.

MARILYN: But my father, Moe, was very strict when I was growing up. You could feel the love in the house but there was not a lot of verbalization. Mother was the scolder and punisher, but if my [step]father said you can't do something, nothing I could say would make him change his mind. Mother I could talk into and out of anything. Luckily, my husbands had consistency as far as the kids were concerned—because I was real wishy-washy. It was never "You're grounded for four days"; it was always "You're grounded for the rest of your lives"—and then I couldn't stand looking at their faces.

JOAN: Your mother mentioned that your kids played "theater" when they were young. So did Shemp, Moe, and Curly.

MARILYN: They did *Cabaret*, and Bradley was no more than four or five years old. He played the part of a pregnant monkey. They put on the whole thing. I'm really proud of all of them. They are all so different. They don't look alike, act alike—they are all very kind, fantastic kids.

JOAN: Do you recall any humorous stories your mother told you about her marriage to Curly?

MARILYN: There was one I recall about the first dinner she ever made for Curly. She made a carp or . . . anyway, it was a whole fish—with the head and the eyes and the tail still on it, and she cooked it and made this gorgeous thing, and she set it on the table, and Curly looked at it and he said, "Hon, I don't think you cooked the fish." She said, "Of course I cooked the fish, of course I cooked the fish. What are you talking about?" And he said, "Then why is it winking at me?"

JOAN: I know I asked you this before, but still, there must be something else you can tell me about what kind of a father Curly was.

MARILYN: I can tell you Curly wasn't a good, bad, or indifferent father. He probably was a terrible father. He didn't make any effort for child support or do anything, and [my stepfather] Moe did not adopt me until I was thirteen. Curly didn't put forth any effort that I know.

JOAN: I know that this will sound as though I'm sticking up for Curly, but he was sick through most of the '40s. I realize, though, that there were several years in there where he was well enough and could have found more time for you.

MARILYN: I remember going to a special school up in Laurel Canyon. It was during the time that it was impossible to find an apartment if you had a child. My mother was just about to marry Moe Diamond. They hadn't bought a house yet, and I had to live in this horrible place. I remember visiting Curly and him visiting me there—and all the stuffed animals. I was about five years old.

JOAN: Your mother told me that some of these stuffed toys were given to you when you were too old for that kind of toy.

MARILYN: I really don't remember. I seem to have blocked a lot of that out. I remember the first time I ever saw Curly in a movie. I went downtown on a bus with some friends. This was just before he died, and it was a vaudeville theater—several acts and then they showed a movie. It was way downtown, like on Main Street. The first time I had ever seen him in a picture.

JOAN: That must have been a once-in-a-lifetime thrill. What did you think of it?

MARILYN: At that time, I didn't like slapstick. It was very unfunny. Even to this day I don't care for comedians. I enjoy it more now.

JOAN: When you were a child, did you ever tell people Curly was your father?

MARILYN: I never told anyone who he was after my mom married [my stepfather] because I thought I was doing him an injustice—my Moe, my father. It was like—if I ever told anybody, it was like Moe wasn't my father. And he was my real father, because anything before that—before I was five years old—was all mixed up.

JOAN: Did any negative things happen to you because Curly was your father?

MARILYN: Oh, absolutely. Subconsciously I know it did. My mother was always concerned about my getting fat [like Curly], and when I would get a little chubby, she'd say, "If you're not careful, you're gonna have a stroke—and die like your father." That was always in my head. I had a lot of fear related to him. Even now, as an adult, I think that maybe I'll die from high blood pressure. I work like a demon at my job and think maybe I'll drop dead when I get home.

JOAN: I'm really a workaholic, too. I love keeping busy. Our grandmother, Jennie, was like that; my father [Moe] was, too, and I imagine Curly was like that. He certainly worked hard in his lifetime. He made ninety-seven two-reel comedies in twelve years and played three months of vaudeville each year. I guess your working hard was inherited from Curly. What kind of work do you do?

MARILYN: I am supervisor for components purchasing. I am in charge of five buyers who purchase electronic components.

JOAN: Did you go to school to learn all of this?

MARILYN: No, for the last thirteen years, I sort of picked it up. At first, I bought military components—a lot more difficult job. You don't have to understand the computer to do my job. I am only buying at the component level.

JOAN: Tell me about your daughter, Andrea. Is she a workaholic too?

MARILYN: Andrea? She's very talented, a great singer. She's a tenor, which is very unusual for a woman. When the kids get together for music, it's great. Someday, when she likes herself, she'll be great.

JOAN: How old is she now?

MARILYN: She's twenty-two. I think she could do something in music if she wanted to.

JOAN: Curly was supposed to have had a fabulous singing voice. In the '20s he used to plug songs, but I don't recall my father mentioning that Curly ever played the piano. He did play the ukulele very well. Do you have any musical talents?

MARILYN: All my kids have wonderful musical talent. It must have missed my generation. I'm horrible. [Pause.] How old was Curly when he died?

JOAN: He was forty-eight.

MARILYN: Both my husbands died at forty-five. After being married nine years, I divorced my first husband, Hal. He died several years later. My second husband, whom I adored, Mickey, died while I was married to him. Hal was seven years older than me, and Mickey was ten years older. They both died at the same age. It broke me up.

JOAN: I feel Curly died young because he didn't take care of himself.

MARILYN: I remember going to Curly's funeral. I was fourteen at the time. My mother was out of town, and I don't recall who took me—my mom was in Las Vegas with my dad [Moe]. It might have been Shemp. I remember going to the funeral and seeing one of the Bowery Boys.

Andrea Server, Curly's granddaughter and Marilyn Ellman's daughter.
Courtesy of Marilyn Ellman

JOAN: Oh, yes—Huntz Hall. Huntz was one of Shemp's best friends. Shemp could not have taken you to the funeral, but he could have gone with you. Shemp never drove a car in his life. You said something about your being angry with Curly. Something about a visit to a therapist. Can you tell me about that?

MARILYN: Oh, it was therapy over being fat and overweight, and we got into going back through the past, and the therapist said, "I want you to remember your real father," and I told him, "I can't really remember a thing." He said, "Sure you can. Think about it." And

I started to think, and one of the things I did remember was fear, because I remember him being paralyzed and lying in bed drooling and having somebody shave him, and I think I was angry at the fact that he was sick. It upset me. And I was probably angry at my mom for keeping him from being a part of me—which he wasn't. I don't know whose fault that was. I remember seeing him, visiting him— and lots of stuffed animals.

Bradley Server, Curly's grandson and Marilyn Ellman's son.

Courtesy of Marilyn Ellman

JOAN: What else do you remember?

MARILYN: I remember Shemp a whole lot. I remember Shemp probably the best—getting silver dollars from him. I remember being afraid and feeling really bad because my father was paralyzed and he couldn't communicate. After he was sick, I used to see him a lot. I remember his wives, and I think there were two. Oh, yes—I remember Valerie. She used to be a nurse or something? I don't ever remember a child. I never knew there was one until . . .

JOAN: Valerie and Curly's daughter, Janie, was born in 1948.

MARILYN: She would be ten years younger than me.

JOAN: You didn't know she existed until when? Ten years ago? How did you find out?

MARILYN: I don't know. I did not know she existed until a Stooges fan told me.

JOAN: Janie's picture was in an issue of the Three Stooges Fan Club newsletter.

MARILYN: I just remember saying, at one point, "I know I have a half-sister."

JOAN: Would you like to meet Janie?

MARILYN: Why, absolutely. I don't look at it as if I'm going to walk up to her and we'll hug each other for this big reunion. But yes, I would like to meet her.

After my lunch and interview with Marilyn, I was utterly fascinated by the thought of Curly having two daughters who had never met. As soon as I returned to my office, I located my cousin Janie's phone number in Maryland, and we spoke for the very first time in our lives. Obviously, we were both nervous, but I'm sure it was more traumatic for Janie, since my unexpected call caught her completely off guard. During our conversation, I asked her if she would join me in a tribute to her father by helping me with a book that I would be writing called *Curly*. Janie was thrilled at the idea, and she and her husband, Frank, agreed to cooperate. I asked Janie to search her memory with regard to her world-famous father and explained that I would call her back in a few days for an interview about her recollections of Curly.

Janie Howard Hanky was born on May 7, 1948, and is Curly's second daughter, with his fourth wife, Valerie Newman. Janie's father died in 1952 when she was three years old, and her mother passed away ten years later when she was thirteen. In 1962 Janie went to live with her mother's sister, Natalie Emery, and stayed with her and her husband, Tom, until she married Frank Hanky in 1972. Janie's education consisted of a year and a half at Christopher Newport University in Newport News, Virginia, and a year and a half in business school. Janie and Frank have one daughter, Kelly, who was born on May 17, 1976.

I called Janie back on March 30 as I had promised and the following is a transcript of our taped conversation:

INTERVIEW

Courtesy of the subject

Janie Howard Hanky

JOAN: What recollections do you have of your father?

JANIE: Well, I remember he used to sing to me all the time. I used to get up on his hospital bed and he'd sing "Oh, You Beautiful Doll." I remember him taking me for pony rides. I recall one time falling in love with this pony. And my father tried to buy the pony, but the man wouldn't sell it. He died when I was three, and I don't recall this part, but I remember my mother telling me that I used to put on his shirt and her high heels and run all over the house, and it used to make [your father] Moe real nervous.

JOAN: Oh, does that bring back memories! My father used to go crazy when I first started to walk. He'd follow me around the room with his hand between my head and the corners of tables.

JANIE: I used to love to dress up, and I'd fall all over the place in those funny high heels.

JOAN: What have your past experiences been when you tell someone Curly is your father?

JANIE: They don't believe me—and they never have. Now I don't really bother to tell many people.

JOAN: In the future it should be a lot easier for you. You can pull this book on Curly out from under your arm and say, "See, there I am."

JANIE: It's funny, but they just didn't believe me. I guess they thought I should be a movie star, too—or live in Hollywood.

JOAN: I can recall being on the phone many times with the secretaries of VIPs I wanted to talk to and getting nowhere. Then I would mention who my father was, and when I'd say, "Joan Maurer, Moe Howard's daughter," they would suddenly be in awe. It wasn't really for me but for my father. I just couldn't believe the reactions.

JANIE: I know. The friends whom I tell say, "Really? You're not really Curly's daughter," and I'll say, "I really am," and now, today, they finally believe me. But I don't tell too many people. Joan, I'll tell you what my father was—I think he was brilliant. I hear people talking—everybody—and they have such respect for his work. I feel now that maybe I was wrong not to tell more people. I feel badly now, because I really am proud of him. But I think because so many times people didn't believe me, I figured, oh, fizzle, why get into it. But I was really proud of him.

JOAN: Do you ever watch Stooges comedies?

JANIE: Not very often now, but as a child I did. It would make me very, very sad. But now I do try to watch them—not a whole lot, but I'm kind of fascinated. Like, his eyebrows and my eyebrows are identical. I think he was generally really funny, but it still kind of makes me sad to watch them too often.

JOAN: I've gotten over feeling sad about my father. It's so incredible— because the average person never gets to see their father on television almost every day of the week. You see your parent aging and then he dies, and suddenly there he is on TV, young and vibrant again.

JANIE: It is really wonderful that we have our parents captured and we can retain this forever. A lot of people aren't that lucky—they might have photos. But there they are, moving all over the screen.

JOAN: Do you like any other comedians?

JANIE: I do like comedians, and they strike me funny, but I like drama more than I do comedy—in movies or things like that.

JOAN: Pick out one comedian whose comedy you enjoy.

JANIE: Oh, gosh—Joan Rivers, Steve Martin, I did like Red Skelton. This is interesting. My father thought that Jackie Gleason was the funniest.

JOAN: Do you like Jackie Gleason?

JANIE: He was really funny, like in The Honeymooners.

JOAN: How do you feel about dogs? Do you like them?

JANIE: Oh, animals. I love animals. I have a dog—part Pekingese and part Yorkshire terrier, and her name is Sally.

JOAN: That's my middle name.

JANIE: Sally? I didn't know that. We did have a cat, Roscoe J. Kitty Kitty, but he was run over. We have some fish . . . but I do love animals.

JOAN: I'll bet your daughter does, too.

JANIE: Not as much as her mother.

JOAN: How about swimming?

JANIE: I love swimming. And I'm building birdhouses. I live out in the country, and I want to make this place like a wildlife refuge—a place for birds. But I do love swimming, and I love aerobics. I love food, and I love the color blue. I like most anything.

JOAN: You love food? But you stay slim. The photos I've seen of you—you're lucky to be able to eat and stay trim.

JANIE: No, I almost have to live on a diet. I love to eat, and when I lose weight I celebrate and go eat a banana split.

JOAN: I know your half-sister Marilyn has a terrible time keeping her weight down.

JANIE: I have to work at it all the time. Food, I love it— eggplant Parmesan, all food—especially if it has something fattening in it.

JOAN: You're just like my mother. Linguini was her middle name. Does your daughter, Kelly, know who her grandfather is?

JANIE: Yes, she thinks it's wonderful. But she is experiencing the same thing as I do—they just don't believe her.

JOAN: That's mean. Does Kelly like to watch the comedies, or are they too violent for her?

Janie Hanky, Curly's daughter; Janie's husband, Frank Hanky; and their daughter, Kelly (1985).
Courtesy of Janie Howard Hanky

JANIE: No, no. She thinks they're wonderful. We took her to the movies once and there was a short with my father in it, and she realized it was her grandfather and she thought it was wonderful. And after that she did tell some people about it.

JOAN: I know what the kids must go through. If it's a youngster saying, "My father is Curly," they think it's her imagination. Now that you're older, I'm sure people will be more apt to believe you.

JANIE: Yes, I've found that in the last few years, too. Because as a kid, they think you might exaggerate.

JOAN: Now that you're older, they know you'd have to be crazy to lie about the fact that Curly was your father. If you're going to lie, you might as well say Elvis Presley.

JANIE: [Laughter.]

JOAN: If you had your choice, would you rather Curly had never been your father?

JANIE: No. No. No. I wish he had lived longer. I wish he had lived longer. He was a wonderful father. The memories I have are wonderful. I think I'm very lucky.

JOAN: How old were you when your mother died?

JANIE: About a month before my fourteenth birthday.

JOAN: Do you recall the date?

JANIE: I think it was April of 1962.

JOAN: Can you recall any other stories that your mother told you about your father?

JANIE: She [Valerie] thought he was so funny. She loved him very much. Oh, she'd love to know what time it was, and he could tell her without looking at the clock—any time of the day. He liked to be on time. I can't remember—they both liked to make plans together, spontaneously. I remember he liked to play the spoons. He would laugh and he was so much fun.

JOAN: I don't know if he was able to get around to dance in those days, since he had had a stroke.

JANIE: I don't know. I think he did. I know he swam a lot.

JOAN: I know my dad loved to swim when he was a young boy. All the Howard brothers except Shemp were swimmers. They lived near the ocean when they were kids.

JANIE: My mother loved the ocean. She liked to play tennis and go horseback riding; she flew planes. She was good at art.

JOAN: How are you at art?

JANIE: I'm just average. No, I don't have the talent there.

JOAN: Did Curly and Val have a good relationship between them?

JANIE: Very, very much so. She wore her wedding ring always. After my father died, I looked at it once and said, "Why is it so skinny on the back?" and she said, "I wore it for so many years that it just wore away." It was white gold, and it was skinny in that one little section.

JOAN: In the years that followed, after Curly died, what did your mother do? Did she work or stay at home?

JANIE: Sometimes she worked. She worked as a draftsman with an electronics firm. She liked to work. My grandfather had a successful restaurant. In fact, my grandfather's history is kind of neat. He came out on his honeymoon from the East Coast to California. He stayed out there and became an assistant director, and then he had a successful restaurant where movie stars would go—John Wayne, he was friends with Richard Arlen and Charlie Foy. My mother managed the restaurant. After my father died, she did work, not only as a draftsman but she sold some of her paintings.

JOAN: Do you have any of her paintings?

JANIE: Just some little sketches, maybe one painting.

JOAN: What name did she paint under?

JANIE: I think just "Val."

JOAN: I understand that after your mother died, your aunt Natalie raised you.

JANIE: Nat and my uncle Tom. It wasn't like all of a sudden I was dropped off at someone's [house]. I didn't [have this problem], because my mother and my aunt were very, very close.

JOAN: Do you feel that because Curly was your father it changed your life in any way? And if so, in what way?

JANIE: No, no. I really don't think so. I'm glad he was my father. The acting and the comedy was only a job. He was funny in real life, too. My mother told me that he just came across funny.

JOAN: Do you feel you got anything positive from your father, something you inherited from him that was kind of special?

JANIE: I know what you mean, but I'm not used to analyzing myself. Some people think I'm real funny, but I never really try to be that way. When I am it sort of comes out—like a mistake.

JOAN: Do you have a job outside the home? Or are you just doing the job I did for thirty-five years, that of housewife and mother?

JANIE: Right now I'm not working.

JOAN: In one of the fan club newsletters it said that you ran a company.

JANIE: I did. I had a balloon company, a balloon delivery company which I loved. Last June my daughter, Kelly, and I were in a serious automobile accident. It took us some time to recover, so I sold the balloon company to the gal I worked with. Now I'm just staying home with Kelly and the dog and the house.

JOAN: Which can be a full-time job.

JANIE: Yes, it can—it really can.

JOAN: Do you sing?

JANIE: Off-key.

JOAN: That's me too. What about your daughter? Can she sing or dance?

JANIE: No, no, nothing out of the ordinary.

JOAN: Your half-sister Marilyn said she has no voice at all, but her three children are musically inclined. But I am so bad!

JANIE: I am too. It's embarrassing. The best I can do is "Happy Birthday"—but that's it.

JOAN: Do you have any desire to meet your half-sister Marilyn?

JANIE: Yeah. I would love to if it ever came to pass. Yes.

The interview ended with both Janie and me delighted that we had finally come together after so many years, even though it was only a phone conversation. Both Janie and Marilyn were thrilled at the thought that, thanks to this book on their father, we had, at last, developed a warm, if belated, kinship.

Even more important to them and to me was my assurance that, come hell or high water, I would see to it that they would finally meet one another in a grand reunion. As this book went to press, I had made the arrangements and looked forward to that meeting with the certainty that Curly, wherever he was, would look down on us with a big grin and n'yuk-n'yuk and woo-woo with delight.*

---

* It took several years, but eventually this meeting did take place. For details, see the afterword, page 181.

CERTIFICATE OF DEATH
STATE OF CALIFORNIA — DEPARTMENT OF PUBLIC HEALTH

JEROME	LESTER	HOWARD

REGISTRATION 1979   REGISTRAR'S 28

2a DATE OF DEATH: JANUARY 18, 1952   3:10

1 SEX: Male   4 COLOR OR RACE: Cauc.   5 Married   6 DATE OF BIRTH: October 22, 1903   7 AGE 48

8a USUAL OCCUPATION: Actor   8b KIND OF BUSINESS OR INDUSTRY: Stage and Screen   9 BIRTHPLACE: New York   10 CITIZEN OF WHAT COUNTRY: United States of America

11 NAME AND BIRTHPLACE OF FATHER: Solomon Horwitz - Russia   12 MAIDEN NAME AND BIRTHPLACE OF MOTHER: Jennie Horwitz - Russia   13 NAME OF PRESENT SPOUSE: Valerie Howard

14 WAS DECEASED EVER IN U S ARMED FORCES? No   15 SOCIAL SECURITY NUMBER: 563-12-6539   16 INFORMANT: Moe Howard

17a COUNTY: Los Angeles   17c CITY OR TOWN: San Gabriel   17c LENGTH OF STAY IN THIS CITY OR TOWN: 1 Week

18 FULL NAME OF HOSPITAL OR INSTITUTION: Baldy View Sanitarium   17d ADDRESS: 8101 Hill Drive

18a STATE: California   18b COUNTY: Los Angeles   18c CITY OR TOWN: Los Angeles (Van Nuys)   18d STREET OR RURAL ADDRESS: 4524 Fulton Avenue

PHYSICIAN'S CERTIFICATION

19c SIGNATURE: R W Edwards MD   DEGREE OR TITLE: 19d ADDRESS: 112 E 9th Los Angeles 15 Cal   19f DATE SIGNED: 4-18-1952

FUNERAL DIRECTOR AND REGISTRAR

20a SPECIFY BURIAL, CREMATION OR REMOVAL: Burial   20b DATE: 1-20-52   20c CEMETERY OR CREMATORY: Home of Peace Memorial Park   3660

22 FUNERAL DIRECTOR: Malinow and Simons, Los Angeles   23 DATE REC'D: JAN 19 1952

CAUSE OF DEATH

25 DISEASE OR CONDITION DIRECTLY LEADING TO DEATH (a): Cerebral Hemorrhage   48

ANTECEDENT CAUSES DUE TO (b): Cerebral Arterio sclerosis   6yr

Over the years many rumors persisted about the assortment of exotic diseases that Curly died from. This should put all rumors to rest once and for all.

7

WHAT MADE CURLY TICK?

A Question-and-Answer Segment with the Author and Dr. John Grenner, Marriage and Family Therapist

After a firsthand relationship with my uncle Curly during my youth, months of research for this book, and dozens of interviews with Curly's family and friends, I still found myself back at square one, trying to understand this very special human being. I had to know what really made Curly, the man, tick.

Many of my interviewees had contradictory thoughts about this superstooge, and much of the Curly puzzle, rather than being solved after these many years, seemed to become more baffling. What effect did mother hen Jennie have on her son during his childhood and in his later life? Did her iron hand have any consequences on his career, his many wives, his early demise? What effect did his brothers have on him, especially my father, Moe?

I was desperate to organize the many puzzle pieces of Curly's fascinating life and career to find out why, after all these years, he continues to affect so many lives.

And then, just a few weeks before my deadline and the shipping of the manuscript to the publisher, necessity became the mother of invention. I remembered my dear friend Dr. John Grenner, an established Beverly Hills marriage and family therapist.

I made a beeline to the phone and had the reward of having John reply that he, like millions of others, was intrigued by the on-screen Curly and would drop everything to help me analyze the offscreen Curly.

When I said, "How about now?" John brought me back to reality. He would first have to review all of my material—over two hundred pages of rough-draft manuscript and all the tapes of my interviews.

I gave John a week to digest everything and nervously awaited his call. When he finally phoned and said, "Let's get together," I leaped into my car and drove to his office on Robertson Boulevard in Beverly Hills.

John made the suggestion that since time was of the essence and since I knew my manuscript backward and forward, it would be best if we discussed all my material on an informal level and taped our discussion on his recorder. I would ask the questions and he would supply the answers, or we would just rap.

The following is a transcript of our meeting:

INTERVIEW

Courtesy of the subject

Dr. John Grenner

DR. GRENNER: After looking over all this material, what strikes me is that Curly, a man well known to millions of people, didn't have any one person who knew him intimately. I think if he walked into my office today, after Jennie had just gotten through with wrecking his marriage, he might say something like "I'm twenty-eight years old. My mother's run my life—all my life. She's just ruined my marriage. I've never really held a real job; she's never let me. And I don't know what I'm going to do about anything.

"I've got two brothers who are very successful, and I love them, but I feel angry because one of my brothers just came home and my mother helped him get into real estate. Sometimes I'm with my mother all day—every day—and she's never helped me make any money. All I ever get to do is drive my parents around like some jerk. Then at night I go dancing, but I can't go dancing for the rest of my life."

Then I might ask him something like, "What's your mother like?" And from what I've read, he'd probably say, "She's always on my case. Whatever I do, it's never enough and it's never right." And then I might say, "How about your dad?" And Curly could say something like, "He's distant, quiet, stays out of Ma's way, goes to Yeshiva, doesn't work a lot and doesn't make much money, either. We don't have much to do with each other." I might ask, "Who do you have a lot to do with?" Curly could possibly say, "I have friends, I like to go dancing, but you know, when I was a kid, I don't know how I did it, but I shot myself in the foot with a rifle. Can you imagine that? And me a dancer. Can you imagine that I'd do something like that? And as for school, forget it. Ma wanted me to be a professional. But I hated school. She went to school more than I did."

JOAN: He certainly was a very sorry young man.

DR. GRENNER: I agree.

JOAN: Your simulated questioning of Curly and your pulling out these few thoughts have started to open doors in my thinking about him.

DR. GRENNER: He strikes me as being very isolated and pressured. Eventually, he acquired problems with weight and high blood pressure, became a workaholic, kind of a type-A personality.

JOAN: Even his wife of two years, Elaine, didn't know him.

DR. GRENNER: I don't think anyone really knew him. He was an enigma. I've been thinking about that reference to his father sitting in the dark and realize that Curly must have gotten a lot of what he knew about being a man from films, newspapers, magazines, and his schoolmates. What he seemed to value in life was mustaches, wavy hair, driving cars, women, dancing, and cursing—but nothing from the heart. I think he must have had a really lonely time of it. Even with his buddies, later in life, when he sat down with his friend Art Seid, for example. Art told me he really didn't know him. He said that Curly would sit down for just a short time and then get up and leave. There are no real intimate relationships that pop up in the interviews. I think really what happened was that he just couldn't commit to relationships on an adult level or even with his daughter. He was always moving on—a kind of a will-o'-the-wisp sort of guy. A loner.

JOAN: And saying things in press interviews like, "Who wants to live long anyway." If he's going from one thing to another and getting bored down the line, what's left for him in life?

DR. GRENNER: I don't know. But you can imagine a man whose trademark in his personal life seems to be ripping a tablecloth to pieces and clicking a pair of teaspoons together.

You know, in almost all of the interviews, that's what people who were close to him recalled about the man. There was really nothing from interview to interview that was as constant as that.

JOAN: That is an interesting observation.

DR. GRENNER: There must have been a great deal of tension that needed to be released.

JOAN: God, yes. And just the idea of ripping cloth to the beat of music.

DR. GRENNER: Perhaps that was why he was never able to read a book. He was so much into his own thoughts. That could account for the problems he had memorizing his lines.

JOAN: Some other interesting facts brought out about Curly were told to me by a close friend of my parents when I first interviewed her three years ago. She told me Curly couldn't contribute anything to a marriage and that his wives probably married him because he was a personality. He had no substance of any kind, and she couldn't imagine him ever saving "I love you" to a woman. She said that Curly always seemed to be in a trance. Here's another quote: "A mental giant he wasn't. I don't think he knew who the president was. He just liked a good time and that was it."

DR. GRENNER: He was very much into his own world.

JOAN: I can see that.

DR. GRENNER: And a man who was raised very clearly with the idea that he wasn't able to handle his own life. Jennie frustrated him at every turn, kept him absolutely under her wing, made sure he had a job to do every day and basically never let him out in the world at all. And then that overprotectiveness was passed on to Moe, and he did the same thing. Curly couldn't help but get the idea that he was incompetent. If you look carefully, you'll see that his on-screen personality is very close to his offscreen personality.

JOAN: He was like a little child.

DR. GRENNER: That's right—unable to make any impact on his environment. It's the environment that was always attacking him, always surprising him.

JOAN: It's fascinating that you came up with this observation. I've received dozens of letters from Curly's fans who feel that his on-screen persona was real, that he was the same type of person on- and offscreen.

DR. GRENNER: I grant you this is all speculation, but look at his first job with the orchestra. There he is up on the podium—the orchestra is attacking him, his clothing is falling apart in front of all those people. That's what he did all the rest of his life—fell apart on the screen as things assailed him.

JOAN: I was thinking about what you said earlier about Curly being overprotected, and I want to read you a page from one of my father's letters to my mother. In the letter, Moe mentioned a suit which he had purchased and which turned out to be too large for him, and he wrote, "The suit is just the thing for my brother Babe—if he is behaving himself." This letter was written in 1924, and Curly would have been twenty-one years old.

DR. GRENNER: I really feel he was viewed as not really able to be trusted with his own life. Another thought—in all your research could you find one close male friend? With his humor, the popularity that he had in the community, it's hard to believe that Curly had no close friends throughout the years.

JOAN: It was interesting that the letter from his girlfriend Ernestine revealed there was no closeness with her either. Her words about him were, "He was just a nice guy."

DR. GRENNER: Yes, a nice guy, alone—and almost completely dependent.

JOAN: Things never seemed to work for Curly, even his marriages: number one, Jennie nixed; number two with Elaine lacked commitment. On reading Elaine's interview, I got the feeling they weren't right for each other. She was a girl from UCLA, and Curly was this crazy guy who couldn't read a book. I recall Elaine's words after she saw Curly on the stage for the first time: "I couldn't believe I was married to that." The only marriage that seemed to have a semblance of happiness for Curly was the last one, with Valerie.

John, another thing came to mind when I was looking over the photographs for the book that were taken on the set of What's the Matador? In the snapshot with director Jules White, Curly almost looks pained as he tries to concentrate on what Jules is saying.

DR. GRENNER: Perhaps he had to use intense concentration in order to keep himself focused. Perhaps it was the pain that he had from his foot showing through.

JOAN: Another thought about Curly's on-screen persona as relates to his offscreen persona, I realize that Curly did follow a script, but he did do a lot of improvisation, and he always reacted in scenes in his own special way.

DR. GRENNER: Life always acted on him and he always reacted to it. He was never able to predict or foresee anything. He could never tell consequences. On film, he'd get into a jam and we'd see him walking into it, but he never saw it himself. And if you ask who needs protecting in this world, it's people who can't see the consequences of their actions. That's why parents watch their kids. They know what happens when you walk in traffic.

JOAN: I don't know if I mentioned it, but Shemp was the exact opposite of Curly: Curly loved to drive, swim; he loved dogs and women. Shemp had these incredible phobias: he was afraid of driving a car, feared dogs—except his own—had apoplexy if he was in water deeper than his bathtub, and seemed to be afraid of his wife—not real fear, but like Sol, he wasn't the boss of his house, either. That reminds me of one of the questions I wanted to ask you. All of the Horwitz brothers had the same parents, then why the great diversity in their makeup? Was this heredity or environment?

DR. GRENNER: Probably a little bit of each. But each son grew up during a different time in their parents' lives.

JOAN: I see what you mean. The parents were at home with the first children, much less so later on. They had no money during their early marriage, and Jennie was wealthy later on. They were happy, then unhappy.

DR. GRENNER: Some of the kids may have escaped the worst of that. But not Curly. It seems to me that, early on, the major skills Curly developed were practiced after Jennie's bedtime.

JOAN: By the time Curly was in his teens, all the other sons had left home and he was alone with Jennie. He was like an only child.

DR. GRENNER: Until reading this material, I don't think I ever saw Curly in this way. You have the parents' marriage, basically based on Eastern European tradition. Theoretically, that's the male in charge—at least in public. Mom may run the show from behind the scenes, but you know there was none of that in the Horwitz family.

JOAN: Jennie was really the boss.

DR. GRENNER: That's right. In Europe, it wasn't unusual for the women to take care of business with the local merchants, learn two or three languages while the men learned Hebrew. Women often took care of a great many transactions in the community outside the ghetto while the men—the "Yeshiva bokers"—studied the Torah. But even with all that, the man was considered the head of his home. In this case we have Jennie functioning in a traditional way, working with the merchants with Sol going to the Yeshiva. But the big difference here is that the tradition of the male on top is absolutely upside down in this household. And my guess is Moe really identified with Jennie and not his father.

JOAN: You're absolutely right. My father idolized Jennie—even loved to cook because of his recollections of helping her cook when he was a very young boy. And then, as an adult, he loved cooking meals for my mother.

DR. GRENNER: It was easy for Curly to fall in with Moe's ways as well. After Jennie died, Moe became Mom. Take a look back into the '20s, when Curly was being raised; that was a very male-oriented society even in the United States, and you can see he really had no males in his immediate environment to identify with. I think this lack of a male model could have been a factor in his going from one woman to another, trying to satisfy his needs.

JOAN: What about Jennie and Sol's relationship to Curly? Was that abnormal?

DR. GRENNER: Well, it certainly wasn't usual for the times. The combination of a passive father and a dynamic, successful working mother must have been somewhat confusing for all the brothers.

JOAN: Curly's brothers Irving and Jack left home even before Moe and Shemp left. Curly was alone—idolizing his show business brothers, dreaming of leaving his mother and joining them on the stage.

DR. GRENNER: In fact, Curly probably would not have gone into show business except for the fortuitous break of Shemp's leaving the act.

JOAN: I never thought of that. I wonder what would have happened to Curly if Shemp had not left the act?

DR. GRENNER: I don't know. It's hard to imagine him as anything else but one of the Stooges.

JOAN: How did shaving his head affect his life?

DR. GRENNER: I'm sure it added to his sense of isolation. Certainly, since his wavy hair was one of his strong points, here again was something else that weakened him in his battle with the world.

JOAN: What was Curly's relationship to Moe? I wonder what would have happened to Curly if Moe had not taken over the role of mother?

DR. GRENNER: I think he would have slid all over the place.

JOAN: I guess he needed that controlling hand.

DR. GRENNER: I agree. Twenty-one, twenty-two, twenty-three years of being controlled and having someone tell you what to do every day, and eventually you're going to get the idea that you can't do anything yourself. Usually, that sets up a kind of rebellion where, on the one hand, you're saying, "God, this is terrible. Someone has to do it for me because I can't do it for myself." And then the other side of you says, "Why the hell can't I do it?" And you push everybody away and start avoiding people just so that they won't interfere with you. And then as your confidence erodes, you find yourself getting sucked back in again, and what you have is a kind of moving in and out of relationships—being too far away is threatening, and being too close is threatening.

JOAN: Did this affect Curly's relationship with women? Was he really equipped emotionally to interact with women on a meaningful level?

DR. GRENNER: I don't think so.

JOAN: My brother Paul wrote in a letter, "Curly could dance with his wives, sing to them, but a relationship with substance seemed beyond his limits. And then, in later life, Curly was insecure about his shaved head."

DR. GRENNER: Yes. I'd buy that. I think he was insecure all along. I know this is out of the blue, but what was Curly doing with a loaded rifle? I couldn't find that in the material.

JOAN: He was on his parents' farm, hunting with a neighbor's boy.

DR. GRENNER: Do you have any idea why he was playing with it?

JOAN: My dad mentioned that the gun had a hair trigger. Curly was holding it in his lap and apparently playing with the trigger.

DR. GRENNER: I don't know. I have some trouble with that. There is an old saying that there are no accidents.

JOAN: I really believe that.

DR. GRENNER: Another question. Was Curly heavy throughout his life?

JOAN: No. In his teens he was very nicely built.

DR. GRENNER: When did he start to put on weight?

JOAN: I don't know exactly, but my guess is starting in his early thirties; he stayed up late, ran around eating out in restaurants all the time.

DR. GRENNER: And drinking—and being down.

JOAN: And you sometimes shove food in your face out of boredom.

DR. GRENNER: It's a sort of compulsive quality. Another thought. Several people brought out that he had pain in his life—both Art Seid and Norman Howard. Isn't it ironic that he shoots himself in the leg and one of his primary loves is dancing? One of the few things he was really good at.

JOAN: Why do people do things like that?

DR. GRENNER: Sometimes people continually sabotage their lives, put obstacles in their own paths.

JOAN: Why did Curly always feel a need for change? New houses, new cars, new dogs, new wives?

DR. GRENNER: I don't think Curly was very comfortable with the way he was and where he was.

JOAN: My cousin Dolly said he was very restless, that he was sweet and loving but not very mature. She said he seemed to need women to soothe this restless quality, not just for sex.

DR. GRENNER: He could have been agitated and restless. I think he hated to be cooped up or to be in one place too long. I think that we can also track that back to his childhood.

JOAN: And here we come with the number-one question. It might be a bit redundant at this point, but do you think that Curly was a very unhappy man—or was this just the normal ups and downs of life?

DR. GRENNER: No. I think he was a very sad person and isolated. I believe that what he portrayed on the screen really represented a theme in his life—that of being put upon, being set up, being betrayed and shown as incapable of mastering his environment in any way.

JOAN: In the end, Curly was always the fall guy.

DR. GRENNER: That's right. He was always on the outside of life, both in the real world as well as in the parts he played.

JOAN: He was always frustrated. What kept him from leading a normal life, one without excesses?

DR. GRENNER: Being depressed, perhaps. You know, in later years he drank quite a bit. Some say to kill the pain in his leg, or perhaps for him it was to make life more bearable. Lots of people make that mistake. Curly was not what you would call a self-starter. He really didn't initiate very much. There is nowhere in the manuscript or the interviews where we see him filling his life with friends, making independent investments, taking pleasure trips, any of those things. What he seemed to do was go to work, have a few drinks, go home, play around a bit with the dogs, back to work again. A very routine kind of existence, and basically a passive one. As if he came out when he was told to and went back when he was finished. A very isolated man.

JOAN: Just killing the hours. Sleep, kill a few more hours—

DR. GRENNER: That's right—a large part of the time.

JOAN: Do you think he had a subconscious death wish or premonition of death?

DR. GRENNER: It's hard to say with any certainty, but the way he ate and the way he drank and the way he worked and drove himself to the point of illness . . . Then there were the accidents with the rifle and the trolley car and Hupmobile. It seems that Curly didn't act in his own best interests. And to the degree that he abused himself, he certainly was self-destructive.

JOAN: I also wondered whether his parents could have ignored him during his childhood, because there were many times that they just weren't around.

DR. GRENNER: You know, there was really no systematic training for Curly. He was like an abandoned kid with nowhere to go. He wasn't in school, he wasn't working with Jennie. And at twenty-three his job was to drive his parents around in their car and that's it. Then your dad comes back home from out of the blue—and there's Jennie right there to help set him up in business. No one really focused on Curly. He was not being taught to be an independent male. Curly was almost like his father, in a sense; he was given no masculine role. He was a kind of gofer.

JOAN: You're right. My cousin Emily said Curly squired her all over New York City in his mother's car. He was Jennie's built-in chauffeur.

DR. GRENNER: It seems to me that Jennie didn't have any interest in helping him develop into a confident person, and I don't think Sol had it in him to bring it off.

JOAN: Why all the silly toilet tricks? Even in photographs Curly would pull his pants down jokingly or pretend he was vomiting, and what about his enjoyment in expelling gas?

DR. GRENNER: You know, that's something that a kid would do. As I said earlier, he learned masculinity from the guys on the corner or the popular media. Even his going down the street and yelling "Hi, toots." It's supposed to be cute, and for sure it's Curly.

JOAN: And "broads," his way of referring to women. A lot of his girl fans wouldn't appreciate that. A woman columnist and fan of the Stooges told me that she didn't care as much for Curly as she did for Moe and Larry. I feel that the female fans liked my dad because he was in control and Larry because he was sweet.

DR. GRENNER: Maybe. The guys certainly like Curly. He makes all those noises and goes crazy. That's the kid in each of us.

JOAN: And the fans would write that he does the things they'd like to do if they had the nerve.

DR. GRENNER: Um-hmmmm.

JOAN: It's strange, but Sol seems to be a blank in his children's lives, and I realize now that Jennie treated him more like a son than a husband—putting him in business, turning over her checks from business deals to him to make him feel important, sending him off to collect the rent money. She would throw him bones.

DR. GRENNER: And she'd throw Curly bones, too. And I think she must have treated both Sol and Curly in similar ways.

JOAN: Her two little boys.

DR. GRENNER: Would it surprise you if Jennie had said to Moe one day, "Moe, darling, when I'm gone, you're going to have to take care of your brother Babe. Someday he's going to be yours and you're going to have to watch over him. You'll have to take care of him, or I don't know what will become of him." My guess is that if this conversation didn't actually take place, it was the message Moe was given over the years.

JOAN: Moe was the next-youngest, and she was not going to ask this of the two eldest who had left home. Shemp was a clown and a kibitzer, and my dad was the serious one. He was more like her.

DR. GRENNER: Yes, and I think Jennie must have recognized this. That's where the strong rapport was. Moe was the mover. He made things happen like she did.

JOAN: I keep wondering why Curly had no close friends.

DR. GRENNER: It does seem strange that a man who was so popular did not have a steady social network. I think Curly was preoccupied—sort of self-centered with little awareness of the needs of the people around him. For example, bringing those stuffed animals to one of his daughters when she was far too old to appreciate them.

JOAN: Oh, yes, Marilyn.

DR. GRENNER: Right.

JOAN: Yes. I can hear him say, "Oh, look—a stuffed dog. I love dogs. I'll get this for Marilyn."

DR. GRENNER: Something like that.

JOAN: A selfish little kid.

DR. GRENNER: I think he was preoccupied with the kind of things that would make him feel good, secure, or take the pressure off him.

JOAN: And Elaine. Curly asking her to come to New York, and when she got there—telling her to go home.

DR. GRENNER: When Curly got something, he often lost interest in it. And, who knows, his plans may have changed, and because his plans changed, he didn't have use for her anymore.

JOAN: What do you feel was his driving need to be a Stooge, or was this just something to do?

DR. GRENNER: I think being a Stooge was the perfect thing. He had that exhibitionist part of him already developed as a show-off kid, so he easily connected when Shemp left the act. I really don't know what else he would have done. There was no other channel open to him other than the ones his brothers provided for him. His choice would not have been real estate, because he certainly wasn't going to go into his mother's business. And he was untrained for anything else, except, I think, becoming a Stooge. But in his own way Curly was a very strong person. His genius on-screen, I think, was his ability to take the frustrating, the unfair, the unbelievable situations we've all confronted in our lives, become thoroughly entangled with them, often unwillingly, sometimes blindly, and survive time after time after time—just as he did in his own life and just as he goes on doing in his films today.

8

AFTERMATH (1980s)

Curly the Cult Hero

I n 1946, after Curly's stroke forced him to leave the act, it seemed as though the Three Stooges dynasty had come to an end. But such was not the case. The popularity of this threesome act and the revenues they were generating could not be ignored by the executives at Columbia Pictures. Although Curly, the catalyst that everyone believed made the act successful, was gone, there was still hope, faint though it was, that Three Stooges films would continue on. And although its magic would never be the same without the superstooge, continue on it did. Ironically, Curly's older brother Shemp, the original Stooge who was replaced by Curly, came back to take his brother's place. Although Shemp was a topflight comic, the act was never the same, but substitution proved better than abandonment, and seventy-seven Three Stooges shorts were produced with Shemp.

Then in 1955, Shemp died suddenly from a heart attack, and the end of the Three Stooges was again at hand. And once again, what seemed the inevitable demise of the act never came to pass. Joe Besser replaced Shemp, and after a few short years, Joe DeRita replaced Joe Besser.

Columbia, in the cases of both Shemp's and Joe Besser's shorts, cut budgets by taking key production scenes from Curly's most successful films and reworking them into new shorts with new titles. As most fans and reviewers seem to agree, these remakes were never quite the same. Curly was a special Stooge, with a special charm and a unique chemistry, and as such he was impossible for anyone to duplicate, no matter how talented they were in their own right.

Columnist Gary Deeb wrote, "Compared to the original Curly [his replacements] were mediocrities."

Jon Matsumoto had his say when he wrote, "All the others remained in Curly's shadow."

Margaret Engel, columnist for the *Washington Post*, wrote, "Curly's antics were an inspiration to our present generation of comics. You could see Curly-isms in John Belushi's work. I'm grateful for Curly for his sense of madcap invention that added a new physical vocabulary to our television comedy."

Film and television actor Barry Pearl stated, "Shemp looked too much like Moe. Joe Besser always looked as though he'd rather be doing it alone. Joe DeRita seemed to be the least commanding and the least funny. In summation, give me Curly, Curly and more Curly."

There is little doubt that millions of Stooges fans are in agreement. It's interesting to note that all of the twelve supersuccessful volumes (three shorts to a volume) of RCA/Columbia's videocassettes were Curly shorts. At almost all of the many film festivals of Three Stooges shorts exhibited in theaters throughout the world, there are merely undertones of mirth when it's a Shemp, Besser, or DeRita film and uproarious, wild cheers when it's one of those films that the fans have nicknamed "Curlies."

And so it should be, for with all due respect to my father, Larry, Uncle Shemp, Joe Besser, and Joe DeRita, Curly was unquestionably the greatest—the most perfect Stooge of all. A superstooge whose unique chemistry made the act so phenomenally successful that it was capable of continuing to entertain thirty-three years after his death.

There is absolutely no doubt that much of the success of the extraordinary current resurgence of the Three Stooges belongs to Curly, the Stooge par excellence, loved by fans of all ages from Maine to Madagascar.

Even the well-known author of the '60s, Jack Kerouac, was a Curly fan and described him in a fascinating paragraph in his book *Visions of Cody*:

"All big dumb convict Curly does is muckle and yukkle and squeal, pressing his lips, shaking his old butt like jelly, knotting his Jell-O fists, eyeing Moe, who looks back at him with that lowered and surly, 'Well what are you gonna do about it?'"

By the 1980s, accolades by the media brought out the fact that Curly had surpassed the Marx Brothers and Bogart and, indeed, become the leading cult hero of the age. Jerome "Curly" Howard, with his shaven head and a larynx that could produce high-pitched squeals and n'yuk-n'yuk noises, even had a song written about him in 1984, "The Curly Shuffle," which sold more than one million copies.

An oil painting (20 inches by 24 inches) by Stooges fan Rhonna Resnick.

The composer of "The Curly Shuffle," Peter Quinn, summed up his reasons for writing his song about Curly and not about Larry or Moe or the Stooges as a threesome. "Because all you have to do," Peter said, "is listen to Curly. His sound effects were incredible. And for such a fat guy, he was wonderfully graceful. He is like a full-grown kid." Quinn went on to say, "Curly is my favorite Stooge and everyone has a little Curly in 'em—dumb but lovable."

And so the distinction of everyone's favorite Stooge has been given to Jerome "Curly" Howard, that manic, whining, graceful, pudgy manchild adored and imitated by millions.

One can easily understand why performers such as Humphrey Bogart, Marilyn Monroe, and Elvis Presley have had their day as cult heroes. They were individual stars who appeared in big-budget major motion pictures with worldwide distribution.

IT DOESN'T MATTER HOW ADVANCED A PHONE SYSTEM IS IF THE WRONG COMPANY INSTALLS IT.

Unfortunately, even the right telephone equipment can go haywire in the wrong hands.

That's why Tel Plus believes the key to a successful communication system isn't only advanced technology.

It's advanced people.

And that's the difference between Tel Plus and other communication companies.

We have experienced, skilled professionals who will design, install and service the perfect telephone system for your business.

People who will analyze your needs, and listen to your wants. And recommend equipment that will satisfy both.

What's more, all of our systems come with this important back-up system: service people who are the best in the industry.

How do you know we can keep these promises? Because we've been keeping them since 1972. As the largest independent telecommunication company in the U.S. with over 65 offices nationwide, we have

over 25,000 phone systems already in place.

So if you're planning on installing a new phone system, or adding to a present one, make sure the advanced equipment you choose comes with this important feature: advanced people.

TEL PLUS ℠
COMMUNICATIONS, INC.
**INTELLIGENT COMMUNICATION BEGINS WITH INTELLIGENT PEOPLE.
CALL 1-800-TEL-PLUS**
A Telecom Plus International Company

1985 ad campaign for TEL PLUS Communications Inc.

Even groups like the Marx Brothers achieved cult status, and the reasons can be readily understood. They also made an extensive series of major motion pictures, but they achieved their cult status as a group with neither Harpo, Chico, Groucho, nor Zeppo ever being singled out as a major cult figure on his own.

Why, then, has Curly Howard been singled out from the group by millions of Three Stooges fans? Why are those millions woo-wooing, squealing "Why soitenly," n'yuk-n'yuking, and imitating all of his many patented mannerisms?

For months I wrote letters to Stooges fans, quizzed others, queried present-day comedians and columnists, and harassed my husband, Norman, who wrote, produced, and directed the Stooges' non-Curly feature films and was also a Curly fanatic.

Over the previous ten years, I had already received thousands of letters from Stooges fans throughout the country. After selling over four thousand of my father Moe's canceled checks (to raise funds for the City of Hope hospital and research center), I received many more letters. I reexamined all of them and realized that they were literally love letters to the Stooges, sent on by doctors, policemen, lawyers, computer experts, white-collar workers, blue-collar workers, even housewives. Uh-uh. These weren't missives from kids; these were creatively composed letters from working adults, "baby boomers" who grew up with a five-day-a-week diet of Stooges and who still retained fond memories of these three zany, lovable childhood companions—and especially of Curly.

When I asked them to explain why Curly was their favorite, the responses were incredible as well as varied. One fan wrote, "Curly *was* the act. There was something special about a grown man who had the capacity to completely inhabit the soul of a child."

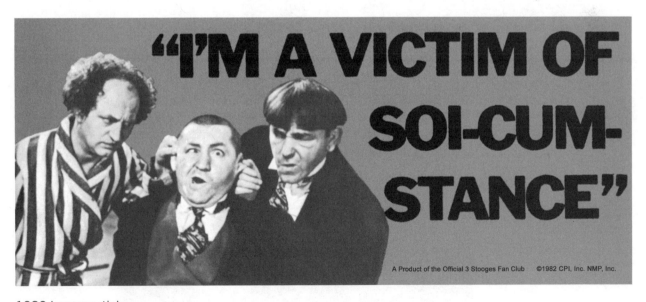

1982 bumper sticker.

CURLY, MOE, AND LARRY FINALLY GET THEIR STAR ON HOLLYWOOD'S WALK OF FAME

All photos from the Joan Maurer Collection

Fans and photographers make up the largest crowd ever to appear for a star unveiling— August 30, 1983.

Batman star Adam West reminisces on playing the lead in the Stooges' last feature film, *The Outlaws IS Coming!*

The author speaks to more than three thousand Stooges fans.

Writer, producer, director Norman Maurer tells the fans of his quarter century with the Stooges. Behind him is Gary Owens, who gathered fifteen thousand signatures to get the Stooges their star.

M*A*S*H star and lifelong Stooges fan Jamie Farr poses for a picture with Moe's granddaughter Jennifer.

Former Stooge Joe Besser tells the fans that Larry, Moe, and Curly are up there watching the festivities.

Joe Besser gives the author a hug. To the left are Norman Maurer and Shemp's daughter-in-law, Geri; on the far right is Larry's daughter, Phyllis.

Photo by Steve Cox

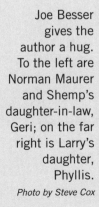

THE THREE STOOGES

The Stooges finally get their star.

Another fan wrote, "Curly was the embodiment of innocence, the little kid in all of us. Yes, Curly was a full-grown man with the soul of a child, dumb, lovable and innocent and he soitenly was the straw that mixed the Stooges into a classic, comedy trio."

A gallery of Curly expressions.

Joan Maurer Collection

Three Stooges van, painted by Bob Borges.   *Courtesy of the artist*

Another fan hit another Curly "nail" smack on its head when he wrote, "[Curly] was the guy who was never smarter than the audience."

A fan from Texas put it this way: "I did love Curly best. The looks on his face, the shyness that came through, sometimes, and then self-assertiveness at others. After watching the Stooges every day for over twenty-five years, I was never once bored by any episode. I could come in from a bad day or have other problems on my mind, or sometimes even feel blue. But one of Curly's 'woo-woos,' 'soitenlys' or 'I'm a victim of soicumstances,' and I was instantly cured."

This letter fascinated me. I couldn't help but wonder whether millions of today's Curly fans were "woo-wooing" or squealing "Why, soitenly" or "I'm a victim of soicumstances" to keep those around them from feeling blue.

I will never forget one particular letter. This fan's name was Stanley Marx, and when he first wrote to me, I discovered that Stanley was a long-lost cousin. His grandmother was my grandfather's sister. After his reply, we had many telephone conversations and a wonderful reunion at a dinner at my home when he came from New York to California for his vacation. Stanley's letter, in reply to my query about how he felt regarding Curly, started off like this:

"Since the author of this communiqué spells his last name M-A-R-X, it is not surprising that I have often encountered the query, 'Relative to Karl or Groucho?' Allow me to assure you that it is always with great pride that I respond, 'No—but a cousin of Moe, Shemp and Curly.'"

Cousin Stanley, a lifelong Stooges fan, went on to write, "If Moe seems the brains of this three-part comedy team, then surely Curly is the heart. Curly's charm is a conglomeration of comedic timing, pathos, empathy and psychological identification between him and the fans. This cupid-like, shaven-headed, child-like man can overcome what appears insurmountable with the ease of a bark, grunt or grimace. Curly honed his talents to a fine comedic edge. [He was] a ballerina with the pantomime ability of a Buster Keaton and the sincerity of a Harpo

RCA–Columbia Pictures videocassette Christmas gift for 1984.   *Joan Maurer Collection*

Marx." In closing, Stanley added, "It seems sad that his genius was not recognized some four decades ago, but, as the saying goes, 'Better late than never.'"

Steve Zodtner, a Birmingham, Missouri, fan, also had a succinct analysis of what made Curly so special when he wrote, "Curly runs the gamut of seemingly endless facial and body expressions: amazement, indignation, puzzlement, tempered ferocity, total frustration and seeming indifference to his environment as events occur around him—he seems to be in his

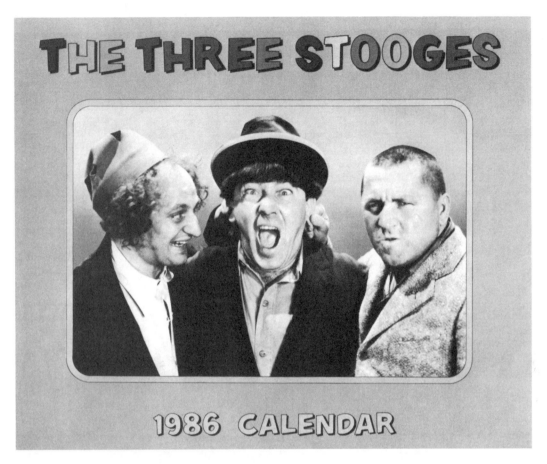

The 1986 Three Stooges calendar by Crabwalk.   *Joan Maurer Collection*

own little world." After describing in detail specific Curly scenes that illustrated the above, he closed with, "He represented the little kid in all of us, the obvious overweight, balding adult exterior and then the dichotomy, the paradoxical child-like attitude about people, places and occurrences. We laugh at his total frustration and temper tantrums, at small tasks gone awry. We laugh at his inability to respond to attacks on his person, intelligence and ability. He is the [Stooges] catalyst—the straw that stirs the drink."

Curly fan Steve Cox wrote, "Donald O'Connor recently admitted to me that he 'stole' something from Curly Howard. You guessed it—a dance step. In the hit movie *Singin' in the Rain*, Donald performs a perfect Curly spin on the floor."

Steven Meltzer, a devout Stooges fan, wrote, "Back then [in the late '50s] Curly was the most riveting and hilarious live action character I ever saw. Here was an ordinary man who had the appearance of my own father but whose being was inhabited with the soul of a five-year-old boy; the 'rebel without a cause,' or for that matter even an excuse."

TV star Anson Williams said, "I loved the Stooges [and] watched them every week when I was growing up. Curly got to me where no one else did. The man was blessed. He had the talent to make you laugh which is the greatest talent in the world. Who knows why—he just had the magic.

Of course, everyone who insulates is smart. But the fact remains that more homes are insulated with Fiberglas Pink than any other insulation.

It's chosen for the ease of handling. The simple installation. And above all, Pink is chosen for its proven money-saving performance.

So next time you're insulating, remember that Fiberglas Pink is the brand chosen by 7 out of 10 people.

As for the other 3, it just seems to go in one ear and out the other.

Nyuk, nyuk, nyuk.

Fiberglas Pink insulation ad.

An ad for Gingiss Formalwear.

Cartoon. Artist: Martin Gerrity.

TO: STOOGE FANS FOR HOPE

PLEASE FIND MY DONATION TO THE CITY OF HOPE,
ATTACHED. I ENJOYED THE ARTICLE IN "NIT&WIT".
THE STAR WAS A LONG TIME COMING!

Tony Pecollo

Illustrated fan letter by artist Tony Pecollo.   *Courtesy of the artist*

From a Curly fan in Milwaukee, Wisconsin, came this gem of an insight into what makes everyone love this cute, chubby clown with a head full of moss: "In the role of the third stooge he was the funniest. Curly was the most physical of the three and was the one who usually got caught with the seat spring stuck to the seat of his pants, or had to chase a wild air hose around in a gas station, or was the poor guy who got stuck with an oyster who spit soup at him!"

TV and screen actor Barry Pearl telephoned me and said, "There was something magical about Curly's humor; and so off the wall. I think that what amazed me the most was that watching him was like watching a live cartoon. He made me realize that I could be a child forever, even if my body grew old."

Columnist Randall Beach wrote, "When the fans hear Curly's immortal n'yuk n'yuk n'yuk, it's like a mating call for the true believers."

Individual passages written about Curly that I culled from hundreds of fan letters sum up why this superstooge has become legend: "A child-like man who can overcome what appears insurmountable odds with a bark, grunt or grimace." "He hones his talents to a fine comedic

COMBUSTION

COMBUSTION is any chemical reaction that gives off heat and light. The *rapid* union of oxygen with any substance is combustion. Combustion is usually thought of only in connection with fire, but it includes many other chemical reactions. Combustion occurs, for example, when chlorine burns in hydrogen gas, or in the burning of any substance in chlorine.

The speed of combustion determines the temperature of the burning substance. If coal burns slowly, the temperature is lower than if it burns rapidly. But the amount of heat given off by the burning of a certain amount of coal is always the same, whether combustion occurs rapidly or slowly. The kindling temperature is the lowest temperature at which a substance burns. The temperature of combustion is the highest temperature reached during combustion. The heat of combustion is the total amount of heat given off when a substance burns. Scientists measure the heat of combustion in calories. See CALORIE.

Spontaneous combustion occurs when the burning substances have not been ignited by a match or some other burning object. Heaps of rags soaked with oil, or piles of coal that contain moisture and other substances, sometimes begin to burn without being ignited. Spontaneous combustion is caused by the rapid union of oxygen with carbon and hydrogen in the oil or coal. This rapid reaction raises the temperature of the rags or coal above the kindling temperature, and the substance begins to burn. RALPH G. OWENS

See also DUST EXPLOSION; FIRE; FLAME; HEAT; OXYGEN.

COMEDO. See BLACKHEAD.

COMEDY, *KAHM uh dih,* is the light and amusing branch of the drama. A comedy usually has a happy ending, unlike a *tragedy,* which usually ends in disaster. The term *comedy* also includes exaggerated forms of comic entertainment called *farce* and *burlesque.*

One of the purposes of comedy is to provide delightful entertainment for theater audiences. Another is to show people how silly they can be. All first-class comic dramatists are serious writers who hope to improve people by showing them their faults in an amusing way. Some of the world's greatest plays are comedies.

Comedies differ from country to country because the senses of humor of the various peoples are apt to be different. For example, French comedy is usually lighthearted and witty. Scottish comedy is *whimsical,* or playful and sweet. English comedy is often clever, but gentle. German comedy may be fantastically exaggerated. Irish is satirical. American comedy is noisy and full of jokes. Comedy often depends on local situations for its appeal. For that reason, a comedy that is extremely successful in one period or place might not be considered at all funny in another. But great comedy always contains elements that are meaningful to all ages.

Comedy developed from ancient Greek festivals in honor of Dionysus (called Bacchus in Rome), the god of revelry (see BACCHUS). In the earliest Greek comedies, a witty fellow simply indulged in ridicule. Later, a plot was added. Greek comedy reached its highest development in the plays of Aristophanes. Two Romans, Plautus and Terence, adopted plots from Greek comedies.

There have been comic playwrights in every period of history when the theater existed. William Shakespeare was the greatest writer of comedy in England in the 1600's. His most famous comedies include *As You Like It, A Midsummer Night's Dream,* and *Twelfth Night.* Molière was the comic genius of France in the late 1600's. In the 1700's, Oliver Goldsmith and Richard Brinsley Sheridan in England and Pierre Beaumarchais in France were important authors of comedy. Masters of comedy in the 1900's include the English playwrights Sir James Barrie, Noel Coward, George Bernard Shaw, and Oscar Wilde; the Americans Philip Barry, George M. Cohan, Moss Hart, George S. Kaufman, William Saroyan, Booth Tarkington, and Thornton Wilder; and the French dramatists Jean Giraudoux and Jean Anouilh. GLENN HUGHES

The WORLD BOOK has a separate biography for each playwright mentioned in this article. See also BURLESQUE; DRAMA; HUMOR; TRAGEDY.

COMEDY OF ERRORS, THE. See SHAKESPEARE, WILLIAM (Types of Plays; table, The First Period; Music).

COMENIUS, *koh ME nih us,* **JOHN AMOS** (1592-1670), was a Czech educator and bishop. His *Orbis Sensualium Pictus (The World of Sense Objects Pictured),* published in 1637, was the first illustrated textbook for children. He favored a broad general education, rather than the narrow training of his day which emphasized the study of languages. He urged the establishment of more schools and universities. Comenius was born in Moravia. CLAUDE A. EGGERTSEN

Screen Gems

Slapstick Comedy for television viewers is provided by The Three Stooges, a well-known burlesque team. Burlesque is one of the most exaggerated forms of comedy.

A page from the *World Book Encyclopedia,* under *C* for *Comedy.*

Joan Maurer Collection

Cartoon by artist Al Jackson.   *Courtesy of the artist*

Cartoon by artist Wayne Koch.
Courtesy of the artist

edge." "A ballerina with pantomime ability." "Moe was the brains, Curly was the heart." "Curly was the guy who was never smarter than the audience." "He was the full-grown man who made all us kids feel smarter than our parents, our teachers and when we grew up—our bosses."

The last two above-mentioned quotes truly zero in on the key factor that made generation after generation continue to love the Three Stooges and especially Curly. There they were, millions of baby-boom moppets, glued to their TV sets, watching adults who screwed up so wildly, so ridiculously, so insanely that every little kid who watched felt superior to and smarter than the full-grown nitwits on their screens—didn't you?

Perhaps it was the Stooges, and especially Curly, who put the "boob" into the "boob tube."

'BATTLE OF WITS'—DIVIDED BY THREE

Cartoon by artist Ralph Reichhold.

Courtesy of the artist

This is Artist Ralph Reichhold's conception of a "tense dramatic moment" in the Three Stooges' act at the Stanley.

Suffice to say, from my layman's point of view, that my uncle Curly was indeed something special in the ranks of show business. Charlie Chaplin, Lou Costello, Groucho, Harpo and Chico, Buster Keaton, Jerry Lewis, Milton Berle, Dan Aykroyd, Eddie Murphy, and Bill Cosby, to name but the tip of the iceberg, are all superbly talented actors and comedians, but none of them were or could ever be a manchild—a silly, chubby, pixie-like, cute, woo-wooing, n'yuk-n'yuking, barking kid like Curly, whose magic somehow captured some special loyalty that, in all probability, is indefinable except within the innermost feelings of the vast armada of the millions of Curly fans who have made him the superstooge.

My hat is off to you, Uncle Curly. You were, and still are, something special: to your family, to show business, to your millions of fans, and especially to me—and none of us will ever forget you.

Cartoon by an unknown artist.

```
                    JEROME (CURLY'S SONG)


          The son of a clothing cutter
          And a dedicated mother
          Dancing in the ballrooms of New York
          Playing ukulele
          Singing for the ladies
          Drifting gracefully across the floor

          A vaudeville band's conductor
          In the shadow of your brothers
          They made you cut your hair and change your name
          And as you sat there crying
          A part of you was dying
          But comedy would never be the same

          Some laugh with you in the morning
          A generation that you've never known
          Some say that they have forgotten you
          But I remember you Jerome

          Your style and sense of timing
          Your ad-lib improvising
          Were something that the world had never seen
          But as we sat there laughing
          None of us imagined
          What life was like for you behind the screen

          The load you tried to carry
          Through the years with Moe and Larry
          Was meant for one less sensitive than you
          Retired from performing
          You'd wake up every morning
          But the laughter of the kids was all you knew

          Some laugh with you in the morning
          A generation that you've never known
          Some say that they have forgotten you
          But I remember you Jerome

          Some say that they have forgotten you
          But I remember you Jerome


                            Copyright © 1981 John Moran
```

A poem to Curly by Stooges fan John Moran of Pittsburgh.
Courtesy of the author

AFTERWORD

Curly's First Marriage: Lost and Found • Marilyn and Janie: Ever the Twain Did Meet

As this second edition of *Curly* goes to press, it has been nearly thirty years since I set out to tell my uncle's life story. One of the frustrating aspects of my research back in the mid-1980s was finding information about Curly's first wife. Answers given to me during my interviews with relatives and friends were like a comedy of errors. One day I heard that our mystery woman was Jewish, on another that she was "definitely not." I heard that she was an older woman, then that she was young and pretty. During my interview with my cousin Margie Golden, she let out a scream: "*Pauline*—that's her name, Pauline."

Years after the first edition was published, out of the blue, I received a letter from a fan. Sadly, I can't recall his name, but if he reads this, I hope he knows how much I appreciated his detective work.

There in glorious black and white was a marriage certificate: on August 5, 1930, the State of New York recorded the marriage of "Jerry Horowitz" to "Julia Rosenthal." Note the incorrect spelling of "Horwitz"—that's probably why I never found it.

It's also worth noting that contrary to the family lore I relied on to flesh out Curly's story, he and Julia were married not in 1929 but the following year. This means that their wedding took place *after* he got his first job in show business, as a guest conductor for Orville Knapp's band, and after he joined his parents on their European vacation. Curly's mother may still have hoped that the trip would distract him from his show business ambitions, and perhaps Curly got married shortly after their return as a way of pushing back against her influence.

● ● ●

While I was interviewing relatives for this book, I realized that my cousin Marilyn (Curly's daughter by his second wife, Elaine) had never met her half-sister Janie Hanky (Curly's daughter by his fourth wife, Valerie). They both said they would be interested, so as I wrote in chapter 6, "Come hell or high water, I would see to it that they would finally meet one another in a grand reunion." I knew that arranging the get-together would be difficult, because Marilyn lived on the West Coast, in California, and Janie lived on the East Coast, in Maryland. Happily, that meeting took place at a Three Stooges convention in Philadelphia over the weekend of July 22–24, 1988.

It was a life-changing experience for the two sisters. Marilyn and Janie have since kept up a correspondence, and I'm so happy that I could be the catalyst that made this come to pass.

Janie (center) and Marilyn (right) on the day they met, with the author and her brother, Paul.

A CURLY FILMOGRAPHY

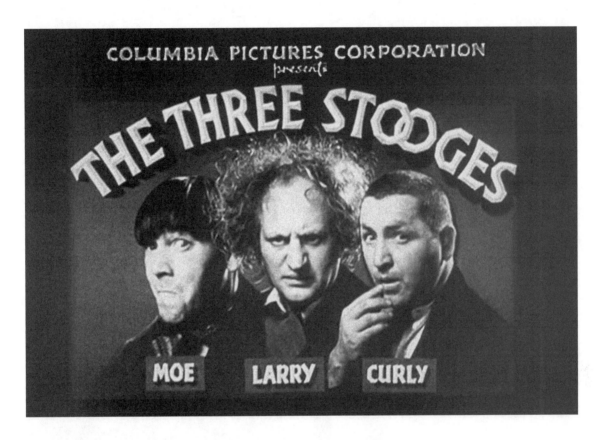

The '30s

Woman Haters
Prod. no. 112 • 1934

Punch Drunks
Prod. no. 116 • 1934

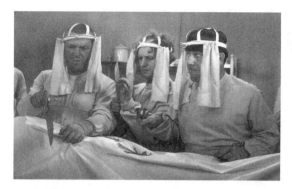

Men in Black
Prod. no. 152 • 1934

Three Little Pigskins
Prod. no. 156 • 1934

Horses' Collars
Prod. no. 159 • 1935

Restless Knights
Prod. no. 160 • 1935

Pop Goes the Easel
Prod. no. 163 • 1935

Uncivil Warriors
Prod. no. 165 • 1935

Pardon My Scotch
Prod. no. 168 • 1935

Hoi Polloi
Prod. no. 207 • 1935

Three Little Beers
Prod. no. 210 • 1935

Ants in the Pantry
Prod. no. 218 • 1936

Movie Maniacs
Prod. no. 213 • 1936

Half Shot Shooters
Prod. no. 225 • 1936

Disorder in the Court
Prod. no. 217 • 1936

A Pain the Pullman
Prod. no. 223 • 1936

False Alarms
Prod. no. 224 • 1936

Whoops, I'm an Indian!
Prod. no. 226 • 1936

Slippery Silks
Prod. no. 221 • 1936

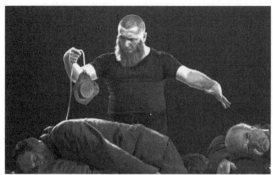

Grips, Grunts and Groans
Prod. no. 259 • 1937

Dizzy Doctors
Prod. no. 263 • 1937

3 Dumb Clucks
Prod. no. 266 • 1937

Back to the Woods
Prod. no. 268 • 1937

Goofs and Saddles
Prod. no. 274 • 1937

Cash and Carry
Prod. no. 400 • 1937

Playing the Ponies
Prod. no. 401 • 1937

The Sitter Downers
Prod. no. 402 • 1937

Termites of 1938
Prod. no. 416 • 1938

Wee Wee Monsieur
Prod. no. 404 • 1938

Tassels in the Air
Prod. no. 420 • 1938

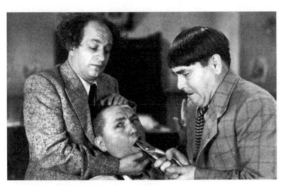

Healthy, Wealthy and Dumb
Prod. no. 422 • 1938

Violent Is the Word for Curly
Prod. no. 423 • 1938

Three Missing Links
Prod. no. 426 • 1938

Mutts to You
Prod. no. 427 • 1938

Flat Foot Stooges
Prod. no. 439 • 1938

Three Little Sew and Sews
Prod. no. 419 • 1939

We Want Our Mummy
Prod. no. 443 • 1939

A Ducking They Did Go
Prod. no. 444 • 1939

Yes, We Have No Bonanza
Prod. no. 438 • 1939

Saved by the Belle
Prod. no. 430 • 1939

Calling All Curs
Prod. no. 445 • 1939

Oily to Bed, Oily to Rise
Prod. no. 449 • 1939

Three Sappy People
Prod. no. 451 • 1939

The '40s

You Nazty Spy!
Prod. no. 472 • 1940

Rockin' Thru the Rockies
Prod. no. 461 • 1940

A Plumbing We Will Go
Prod. no. 462 • 1940

Nutty but Nice
Prod. no. 465 • 1940

How High Is Up?
Prod. no. 458 • 1940

From Nurse to Worse
Prod. no. 468 • 1940

No Census, No Feeling
Prod. no. 474 • 1940

Cookoo Cavaliers
Prod. no. 455 • 1940

Boobs in Arms
Prod. no. 486 • 1940

So Long Mr. Chumps
Prod. no. 484 • 1941

Dutiful but Dumb
Prod. no. 485 • 1941

All the World's a Stooge
Prod. no. 487 • 1941

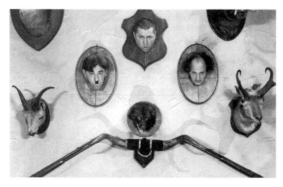

I'll Never Heil Again
Prod. no. 500 • 1941

An Ache in Every Stake
Prod. no. 488 • 1941

In the Sweet Pie and Pie
Prod. no. 482 • 1941

Some More of Samoa
Prod. no. 511 • 1941

Loco Boy Makes Good
Prod. no. 510 • 1942

Cactus Makes Perfect
Prod. no. 513 • 1942

What's the Matador?
Prod. no. 519 • 1942

Matri-Phony
Prod. no. 527 • 1942

Three Smart Saps
Prod. no. 532 • 1942

Even as IOU
Prod. no. 507 • 1942

Sock-a-Bye Baby
Prod. no. 539 • 1942

They Stooge to Conga
Prod. no. 533 • 1943

Dizzy Detectives
Prod. no. 529 • 1943

Spook Louder
Prod. no. 549 • 1943

Back from the Front
Prod. no. 522 • 1943

Three Little Twirps
Prod. no. 551 • 1943

Higher Than a Kite
Prod. no. 568 • 1943

I Can Hardly Wait
Prod. no. 570 • 1943

Dizzy Pilots
Prod. no. 555 • 1943

Phony Express
Prod. no. 569 • 1943

A Gem of a Jam
Prod. no. 575 • 1943

Crash Goes the Hash
Prod. no. 4010 • 1944

Busy Buddies
Prod. no. 4001 • 1944

The Yoke's on Me
Prod. no. 571 • 1944

Idle Roomers
Prod. no. 4013 • 1944

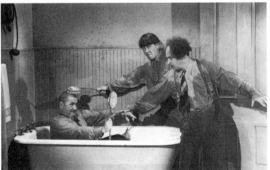

Gents Without Cents
Prod. no. 4020 • 1944

No Dough Boys
Prod. no. 564 • 1944

Three Pests in a Mess
Prod. no. 4022 • 1945

Booby Dupes
Prod. no. 4006 • 1945

Idiots Deluxe
Prod. no. 4030 • 1945

If a Body Meets a Body
Prod. no. 4033 • 1945

Micro-Phonies
Prod. no. 4044 • 1945

Beer Barrel Polecats
Prod. no. 4045 • 1946

A Bird in the Head
Prod. no. 4043 • 1946

Uncivil War Birds
Prod. no. 4050 • 1946

The Three Troubledoers
Prod. no. 4046 • 1946

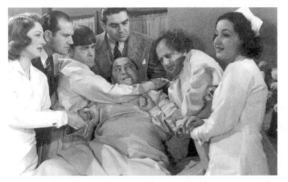

Monkey Businessmen
Prod. no. 4058 • 1946

Three Loan Wolves
Prod. no. 4053 • 1946

G.I. Wanna Home
Prod. no. 4063 • 1946

Rhythm and Weep
Prod. no. 4057 • 1946

Three Little Pirates
Prod. no. 4067 • 1946

Half-Wits Holiday
Prod. no. 4056 • 1947

Curly's Credits Other Than His Ninety-Seven Three Stooges Shorts

Nertsery Rhymes
MGM • 1933

Beer and Pretzels
MGM • 1933

Hello Pop!
MGM • 1933

Plane Nuts
MGM • 1933

Turn Back the Clock
MGM • 1933

Meet the Baron
MGM • 1933

Dancing Lady
MGM • 1933

Myrt and Marge
Universal • 1933

Hollywood on Parade No. B-9
Paramount • 1934

The Big Idea
MGM • 1934

Fugitive Lovers
MGM • 1934

Hollywood Party
MGM • 1934

The Captain Hates the Sea
Columbia • 1934

Screen Snapshots Series 13 No. 5
Columbia • 1934

Screen Snapshots Series 14 No. 6
Columbia • 1935

Screen Snapshots Series 15 No. 7
Columbia • 1936

Screen Snapshots Series 18 No. 9
Columbia • 1939

Screen Snapshots Series 19 No. 5
Columbia • 1940

Screen Snapshots Series 20 No. 3
Columbia • 1940

Screen Snapshots Series 21 No. 3
Columbia • 1941

Screen Snapshots Series 22 No. 8
Columbia • 1943

Start Cheering
Columbia • 1938

Time Out for Rhythm
Columbia • 1941

My Sister Eileen
Columbia • 1942

Rockin' in the Rockies
Columbia • 1945

Swing Parade of 1946
Monogram • 1946

Hold That Lion!
Columbia
Prod. no. 4087 • 1947
(Curly played a cameo role in this Shemp short)

ALSO FROM CHICAGO REVIEW PRESS

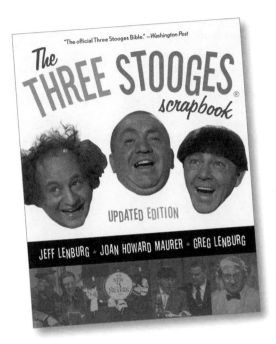

**The Three Stooges Scrapbook
Updated Edition**
Jeff Lenburg, Joan Howard Maurer,
and Greg Lenburg
978-1-61374-074-3
$22.95 (CAN $25.95)

For more than fifty years—in two hundred comedy shorts, twenty-five feature films, and thousands of television, onstage, and personal appearances—the Three Stooges dished out their classic comedy mayhem to the delight of audiences of all ages around the world. And for the last thirty years, one book has given fans the details they crave: *The Three Stooges Scrapbook*.

This lovingly assembled tribute to those cinematic clowns is a meticulously researched and written account of every aspect of the Stooges' lives and careers, copiously illustrated with more than four hundred photographs and illustrations throughout. It is without doubt the most accurate and complete account of the Stooges' career and history ever written.

The only book to feature exclusive interviews with Stooges Moe Howard, Larry Fine, Joe Besser, and Joe DeRita and family members and friends, this authorized history is jam-packed with things Stooge fans want to know: intimate biographies; an in-depth, complete team history; information on Three Stooges merchandise, comic books, record albums, television appearances, and impersonators; and a filmography with details on every one of their films.

Now updated, *The Three Stooges Scrapbook* provides the most comprehensive coverage of the trio to date, with a stunning wealth of material including personal memories and reminiscences, findings and revelations, historical facts and tidbits, and other addenda that will delight fans of all ages.

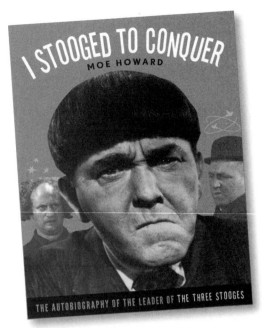

I Stooged to Conquer
The Autobiography of the Leader
of the Three Stooges
Moe Howard
978-1-61374-766-7
$19.95 (CAN $21.95)

Also available in e-book formats

Head Stooge Moe Howard's career stretched from the age of eleven, when, in his first film role, he played a bully in an orphanage, to the age of seventy-seven, when he died while finishing this book. In *I Stooged to Conquer*, he tells the intimate story of the man who made some of the zaniest flicks of all time.

Born into a working-class family in Brooklyn, Moe transformed his real-life experiences of getting into mischief with his brother Shemp into the plots that would have millions rolling in the aisles. From childhood, Moe's sole ambition was to perform—whether it was joining the Anette Kellerman Diving Girls, plucking a ukulele on the beach, or playing a half-wit on a Mississippi showboat. But he only found success when he joined with Shemp and Larry Fine to play, as the *New York Times* put it, "three of the frowziest numskulls ever assembled."

As the brains behind the Three Stooges, he went on to act in over two hundred of their movies, introducing his little brother Curly into the act when Shemp departed, and, after Curly's death, partnering again with Shemp, and then with Joe Besser and finally Joe DeRita.

I Stooged to Conquer (originally published as *Moe Howard & the 3 Stooges*) is Moe Howard's self-penned, no-holds-barred story of the ups and downs of his life, ranging from personal family tragedies to career mishaps and triumphs. It overflows with the easygoing charm, generosity, and inspired lunacy of the "wise guy" behind America's most successful comedy trio.

CHICAGO REVIEW PRESS

Available at your favorite bookstore, by calling
(800) 888-4741, or at www.chicagoreviewpress.com